Carvers' George

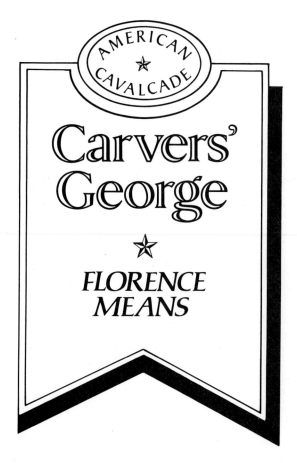

AMERICAN CAVALCADE

Carvers' George

★

FLORENCE MEANS

MARSHALL CAVENDISH
CORPORATION

GREY CASTLE PRESS

Published by Grey Castle Press, Lakeville, Connecticut.

Marshall Cavendish Edition, North Bellmore, New York.

Published in large print by arrangement with Houghton Mifflin Co.

Library of Congress Cataloging-in-Publication Data

Means, Florence Crannell, 1891–
    Carvers' George / by Florence Means.
        p.   cm.— (American cavalcade)
    Reprint. Originally published : Boston : Houghton Mifflin, 1952.
    Includes bibliographical references and index.
    Summary: A biography of the black scientist famed for agricultural research that revolutionized the economy of the South.
    ISBN 1-55905-075-6 (lg. print)
    1. Carver, George Washington, 1864?—1943—Juvenile literature.   2. Afro-American agriculturists—Biography—Juvenile literature.   3. Agriculturists—United States—Biography—Juvenile literature.   4. Large type books.   [1. Carver, George Washington, 1864?—1943.   2. Agriculturists.   3. Afro-Americans—Biography.   4. Large type books.]   I. Title.   II. Series.
[S417.C3M33 1991]
630'.92—dc20
[B]
[92]
                                                                                      90-49179
                                                                                           CIP
                                                                                            AC

ISBN 1-55905-075-6
        1-55905-100-0 (set)

Photo Credits:

Cover: AP/Wide World
George Washington Carver National Monument—pgs. 11, 24, 55, 91, 123
Tuskegee University Archives, Tuskegee, AL—pgs. 80, 86, 111
The Bettmann Archive—pg. 98
UPI/Bettmann Newsphotos—pg. 137
AP/Wide World—pg. 156

Contents

★

1

I Want to Know

THE TIME was the late eighteen-sixties. The place was the Ozark plateau, shadowy with tall trees, bright with wild flowers. The chief character was a boy all alone outside a country schoolhouse.

It was a homely schoolhouse, and nothing to brag about. Inside were long benches, with boards fastened in front of them for desks. On the wall near the teacher's table was a homemade blackboard, and above it hung a threatening hickory stick. Near the door stood a bench with water bucket and gourd dipper, and one wall was studded with nails where hats, coats and lunches were hung. Pupils crowded the benches, the girls with pinafores, homespun dresses, ruffled panta-lets, their hair in braids and frizzed bangs. The boys wore homespun, too, and stout copper-toed boots if they did not go barefoot.

Through the open door the boy outside could

hear the squeak of slate pencils on slate. He could see and hear the teacher teaching and the pupils reciting.

"A!" said the teacher, making the letter on the blackboard. "And B. Say them after me, scholars: A, B. Now put them together and read: A, B, Ab."

The boy outside was not much larger than these primer children. He was about eight-year-old size, but his expressive face seemed much older. Whatever his age, you could guess by looking at him that he was small for it. He was that style of boy: thin as a new colt, with hands too large for his arms, feet too large for his chicken-bone legs, and big, shining eyes that took in everything around him.

Was he playing hooky? Was he thinking himself lucky to be free in the sunshine while the boys and girls inside yawned and stretched on the hard benches?

No, he would gladly have traded a few hours of the outdoors each day for those hard benches, those dusty smells of chalk and slate, even with the sting of the hickory stick thrown in. He had spent all his years learning about trees and flowers, animals and birds. He already knew more about them than the teacher did. It was this other knowledge that he had been unable to get: the kind locked away in books.

The one book he owned was a blue-backed speller, which he prized above all other belongings. He kept it covered with brown paper which he had ironed out smooth. Little by little he had learned the letters in it. Some he had got by listening outside the schoolhouse. Some he coaxed from busy Aunt Susan; some from the other children. He collected letters as he collected marbles and pebbles, but it was harder work. It would have been easy if he could have spent his days inside that schoolroom, but if he had stepped in, every head in the room would have turned to stare. The teacher would have said, "Better scamper home, George."

Why was there no place for him in that country school? It was not because he was an orphan, nor because he was frail and did not grow like other children. It was not because his bad throat had given him a stammer that made his speech hard to understand. It was only because he was a black child in a white country.

In Missouri, as in most other states at that time, black children could not attend white schools. In all parts of the South schools for blacks were springing up, but here in southern Missouri there were so few blacks that it did not seem worthwhile to have a school for them. The state must struggle to educate even its white children. The war just past had destroyed school-houses, and the wealth to maintain them, and Missouri found it hard to rebuild.

That was why "Carvers' George" lurked outside, watching and listening.

How had he been orphaned? Why was he "Carvers' George," with no surname and no birthday? Here is the story.

George was born, probably in January, 1860, in the Missouri Ozarks, near the little town of Diamond Grove. His parents were slaves, his mother belonging to Moses and Susan Carver.

The Carvers were German farmers, Moses a breeder of fine horses. Though thrifty and hardworking, they found the chores on the pioneer farm too heavy, since they had no children to share them. So, while opposed to slavery, Uncle Moses did buy Mary, a girl of thirteen years, to help Aunt Susan.

Mary was well loved in the Carver home, where she proved industrious and honest. She was keen-minded besides. Although she had never been taught to read, she could remember and find the exact page and line in the *Almanac* from which a recipe or fact had once been read aloud in her hearing.

Since the Carvers loved Mary, they welcomed her children, who were born after she had been with the Carvers nearly twenty years. Uncle Moses must have sighed with pleasure at sight of

Moses Carver, George's foster father, was a German home-steader in southwestern Missouri. In 1855 he purchased Mary, a 13-year-old slave. Mary gave birth to George in 1864 or 1865; the identity of his father was never known for sure.

that first baby, big, brown and dimpled. Little Jim could soon help with light chores. Mary's next boy was very different. Poor and scrawny as an unfledged sparrow, his thin neck would not hold up his large head, covered with close-pressed silky black curls.

Sorrow came early to Mary's cabin, near the Carver house. The children's father had belonged to a neighbor, and had come to see his family as often as he could get away from work. Now he came no more. While hauling wood with his master's ox-team he was accidentally killed. From babyhood Mary's boys were half-orphans.

Still deeper tragedy was to strike them.

For years border raiders had terrified the lonely Ozark farms, swooping down to steal horses, cattle, and anything else they could find. Lashing his sweating horse onward through the lonely dark, a messenger would ride the woods to warn farmers that raiders were heading their way.

Moses Carver had already suffered at their hands. Plenty of ne'er-do-wells hated him and his wife for being "foreigners," for working from dawn till dark, and for making a modest success in the new country. Yet, though Moses Carver had reason to know their hate, he did not expect the misfortune which was yet to befall him.

One winter night he and Aunt Susan were startled by screams from Mary's cabin. Grabbing his heavy gun, Uncle Moses raced from the house. Already horses were pelting away with a muffled rain of hoofs on the dirt road. When Uncle Moses dashed, breathless, into the cabin, he found it empty except for little Jim. The raiders had stolen Mary, with the sick baby nestling in her arms.

The Carvers were shaken with sorrow for Mary and for frail little George, already ill with whooping cough and now exposed to the winter night. Uncle Moses galloped after the kidnapers, but soon lost their trail. Next day, searching frantically for clues, he had hopeful news from a bushwhacker, one of the guerrillas who "whacked the bush," fighting in the rough wooded country. This guerrilla told Carver that he knew where the stolen slaves were being held.

Uncle Moses smashed fist into palm. "You bring them home once," he shouted with his German turn of speech, "and forty acres good farm land I give it you. Yes, and a race horse, also."

The bushwhacker went posthaste on his mission.

Day after day as she worked in the lonely house, Aunt Susan's heart jumped whenever she heard horses' hoofs on the road. Day after day Uncle Moses hurried through his chores, always listening for hopeful sounds.

When at last the bushwhacker cantered up to the gate, Aunt Susan rushed out, Uncle Moses following. Both stopped short. No smiling brown Mary rode behind the man. While they stared disappointedly, he explained. The raiders and Mary were gone when he reached the place where he expected to find them, and though he rode hard he could not overtake them. They had crossed the state line and lost themselves in the wooded Arkansas hills.

''We shall find Mary—never!'' Aunt Susan whispered.

''You ain't got a chance,'' the bushwhacker agreed glumly. ''And I reckon this little tyke won't pull through. They'd left him behind with some womenfolks. Throwed him away, really. Them raiders wouldn't fool with him.'' Lifting a bundle of dirty rags from a saddlebag, the bushwhacker held it out to Aunt Susan.

Silent with surprise, she unrolled the cloth and peered into the tiny dark face of Mary's baby. With lips and closed eyelids blue, he looked more than ever like a newly hatched sparrow. As she leaned closer to see whether he was still alive, the bundle heaved slightly and gave a cough. Sobbing, Aunt Susan ran into the house with him, warmed and sweetened a cup of milk, and dropped it by spoonfuls into his mouth.

Outdoors, Uncle Moses steadied his voice to

bargain. Certainly the bushwhacker could not expect full pay for fetching back only the baby, and him more dead than alive. The two men agreed on the racehorse as a proper price, and the guerrilla led it away.

Uncle Moses went into the house grumbling, "A horse worth three hundred dollars for a child worth not three cents already!" Yet he bent anxiously over the baby in his wife's arms, and he warned the sturdy Jim sharply, "Keep those fingers from your brother's eyes out, or I whale you good."

Aunt Susan used all her skill to save the baby who had been thrown away. Coming to see him, the neighbors shook their heads. "With such a start he wouldn't ever be worth shucks, Mis' Carver, even if you could pull him through." "Looks like he has to fight for every breath when he gets those coughing fits. But I'll say this for the young 'un: he's got a heap of fight in him."

The whooping cough had grown worse with neglect and exposure, but little by little he recovered from it. Aunt Susan was proud when at last he could hold up his head on his thin neck and follow every move she made with his wide black eyes. The neighbors, though, continued to shake their heads over him as he grew out of babyhood.

"Didn't we warn you?" they said. "Why, he

can't even talk so you can make out what he says. The child isn't all there.''

The Carvers knew better. George was smart as a whip. As soon as he could toddle he began to do everything Aunt Susan did. His thin little hands, so unlike Jim's dimpled ones, washed and wiped the dishes without dropping a single one, and it was funny to see him carefully run a fold of dish towel between the three steel tines of one of Aunt Susan's table forks.

From the first he helped Aunt Susan, while Jim helped Uncle Moses. The Carver house was made up of two one-room cabins connected by a dog-trot, a roofed open part used like a porch. The larger cabin was for company, and the Carvers lived in the smaller one, with Jim and George. The boys slept on a tick stuffed with straw or cornhusks, doubtless in the loft overhead.

The cabin held a rope-bottomed bedstead, made up with a great feather bed, goosefeather pillows and pieced quilts. It held a cross-legged table and stools, a cupboard and two spinning wheels. It had no modern conveniences, not even a cookstove. And it was so crowded that it was hard to keep perfectly neat, as Aunt Susan wanted it. The job kept two people busy. While still small, George learned to do all kinds of work. He could dip candles and churn, cook, help smoke meat in the fragrant smokehouse, wash and iron, and mend clothing and shoes.

In those days farmers' families had to raise or make everything they used, even shoes and stockings. Aunt Susan was not skillful in knitting heels, nor Uncle Moses in stitching leather smoothly. When puckered socks and rough boots combined to blister Uncle Moses's heels, he took his knife and hacked out his wife's bunchy knitting. Aunt Susan scolded him for his wastefulness, and gave young George the socks to darn. When he had mended them, so perfectly that they could not have hurt a baby's skin, he did such a tiptop cobbling job on the boots that Uncle Moses had happy feet again.

By watching Aunt Susan, George taught himself to knit and crochet. From long, strong feathers out of the poultry yard, he made knitting needles and a crochet hook. When Aunt Susan pieced quilts and embroidered, he imitated her so cleverly that she let him have good material instead of waste pieces, and they worked together. Soon he was drawing original patterns for her needlework, designs that none of her neighbors could equal.

George was no different from other boys, however, in wanting to get through his chores and away. One churning day when the butter was unusually slow to come, he had important matters on his mind: eggs about to hatch in a nest high in a walnut tree, and fish to watch in the "branch" which ran, clear and deep, through the Carver place. He couldn't slip away before the butter was made, for Aunt Susan was keeping an eye on him while she did the washing. Finally, when she was out of sight for a minute, George tiptoed to the clothes-boiling kettle, dipped out a gourdful of hot water and poured it into the churn. When Aunt Susan bustled back, he was working the dasher with the most innocent expression in the world.

"Butter's coming!" he piped in his thin, high voice. And pretty soon he peeped in and cried, "Butter's come, ma'am!"

"What makes it so pale?" Aunt Susan wondered, looking suspiciously at the butter. "Very white it is, George."

"Is it, ma'am?" George asked gravely. "You said I could go when the butter came, ma'am."

Mrs. Carver poked the soft white lump doubtfully and said, "Well, run along with you, then."

He did not always get off so easily. One day the Carvers went to town, leaving George to do the evening chores. He played too long, and when he hurried home the house and barn were dark. Hastily he lighted the one big oil lamp, pride of the household, carried it to the barn and fed and watered the stock by its glow. The Carvers came home before he was through and Uncle Moses gave him a whipping which he never forgot, for the lamp might easily have set the buildings afire.

Most of his whippings were slight affairs, because he was so small, and because, he often said afterward, he yelled so loud that even Uncle Moses hadn't the heart to strike hard.

In play, also, his small size was sometimes an advantage. Though he could not run as long as boys with better wind and stronger legs, he was quick as a rabbit, and could wriggle through cracks and hide in holes that stopped most of the children.

He liked playing with other boys, but still better he liked his own lonely amusements in woods and fields. Great elms and walnuts pushed in on the pasture near the house, and persimmons, haws, oaks, filled the farther woods. The rosy redbud was glorious in springtime, and the dogwood with its four-petaled blossoms like great white stars.

There were animals to watch and tame: squirrels, foxes, possums, civet cats, and skunks with pretty babies like small copies of themselves.

He was always finding treasures: flowers, moss, pebbles, butterflies, and bugs. As he roamed, he nibbled the sweet white ends of

grasses, pulled from their green sheaths, or the
bark and savory mitten-shaped leaves of the
sassafras, or the berries he knew were not poi-
sonous.

He early learned the herbs which Aunt Susan
used for medicine. In those days farm women did
their own doctoring and medicine making. So
George brought Aunt Susan mint and mustard,
jimson and sassafras, gentian and blue flag, to be
hung from the rafters to dry. He brought home
dock, lambs'-quarters and tender young dandelions, also, to go into the fireplace kettle for
dinner.

Aunt Susan welcomed the herbs and greens,
but not the boy's messy collections of flowers,
pebbles, and moss. Still worse were the toads,
which he loved and sometimes took to bed with
him. Every time he came home from a ramble she
stopped him, saying, "Now, George, what you
got this time? Turn out your pockets, sir."

According to Aunt Susan, the crowded cabin
had no room even for his plants, and that was a
grief to the boy, who loved them as other children
loved their playthings. Long before he could talk
plainly enough for other human beings to understand him, he crooned to his plants as if they were
people. And though he could not keep them in
the house, he managed to bring his green pets
through the winter. Under the forest trees he dug

a small cellar, where he set the potted plants, covering them warmly. On mild, bright days he lifted off the covering, gave the green babies sunshine, and pruned and doctored those that drooped.

How had he learned to doctor them? The Carvers answered his questions when they had time or knew the answers, but he soon was wiser about growing things than they. They laughed at him when he anxiously showed them some queer bugs in an apple tree. They stopped laughing when the tree turned yellow and lost its fruit, evidently because of the bugs George had found.

Though his fragile hands were black, they had "green thumbs," and could make plants grow and thrive. The neighbors called him the Plant Doctor, for he trotted from house to house, looking over the geraniums and begonias in their windows, repotting some, loosening the earth around others.

His own knowledge did not satisfy him. The big-eyed child would squat before a geranium and frowningly ask, "Why is one pink and another white? Why does the begonia have shiny leaves and the geranium not?"

No one could answer his questions. He seemed to be the only person in his world who wanted to know; just as he was the only one who saw things like the bugs in the apple tree. He took the difference more or less for granted, like the difference in color that kept him from going to school.

He wanted to do, as well as to know. He whittled. He made horsehair chains and little fiddles. When he first saw a painting and learned that it had been made by a person, he declared, ''If somebody put those flowers on paper, so can I!'' So he made brushes from feathers, colors from berry juice, walnut hulls and grass, and painted his first pictures on scraps of tin and wood.

In the back of his mind a big plan was growing. Maybe this dream began one day when he went to Diamond Grove for an outing.

Uncle Moses was not cruel, though he was strict. Jim and George must do their chores and mind, but he wanted them to be happy. So he sometimes let them go to town and spend the half-pennies, pennies, and two-cent-pieces they earned and saved. He thought two boys were twice as likely to get into mischief as one, so he let Jim go one time and George another.

On one of these lone journeys George had the shock of his young life. He was strolling along, looking, as usual, into the small windows of the general store, which seemed to him big and bright and crowded with treasures. And suddenly, amid the townspeople and farm families he was used to seeing, he caught sight of something that amazed him. "I saw a big—ugly—*black man!*" he told Aunt Susan, when he had run home on shaking legs. He was so scared that he did not even spend the coppers tied up in his pocket. Except for his own family, he had never before seen a black man.

He began to think about the other blacks scattered over the country. There must be other hearts like his, aching for school. While he was still small he decided that he would have a school, as soon as he grew up. He would teach them reading, writing and numbers and more. He would also teach them to sew, knit, make shoes, read and paint. He must learn to do everything himself, so that he could teach them everything.

There was one great difficulty. The hurrying years gave him little chance to learn reading, and no chance to learn writing and arithmetic. Slowly the state was rebuilding its school system, but it did not yet attempt schools for its few blacks. However, Neosho, a town a few miles from Diamond Grove, had such a school, and George made up his mind to attend it. Sadly the Carvers gave their consent. Emancipation had come, and George was no longer a slave, no longer their property.

He was now ten years old or a little more. He had no money. He knew nobody in the strange world to which he was going. But he had a great

As a young boy, Carver was often excused from his farm chores because of a chronic respiratory illness. Instead, he helped with light house-work and explored the woods.

faith. He believed that if anybody could do anything, so could he. He believed that you can make
what you want out of what you have.

What did he have? Skill in a score of household
crafts. Friendship with the earth's flowers, trees,
birds, animals. A frail, stumbling body. A great,
courageous mind and spirit.

He said good-bye to the Carvers and the
rollicking Jim whom he loved. Uncle Moses
scrowled, to hide how sad he felt, and Aunt
Susan cried. They hated to lose George, for the
child was a valued member of their household.

All alone, George Washington Carver trudged
out into the world to seek his fortune. And anybody in that world would have said that he did
not have the smallest chance of finding it.

I Can Do It, Too.

CARVERS' GEORGE made a strange picture as he trudged along the dusty road. Aunt Susan had cut down one of her husband's old suits for the small adventurer, and his spindly body was almost lost in baggy folds that crept down toward his bare toes.

George was not troubled about his looks. He was wondering what kind of people he would find in Neosho, where he would sleep that night, and he was beginning to get hungry.

Neosho, when he finally reached it, seemed big and strange to a boy who had seldom left his home neighborhood. As he walked up and down its confusing streets he felt, for once, not a bit older than his ten or twelve years.

As soon as he finished the lunch he carried, he scouted round the town till he located a stable with an open loft door. At dusk he climbed in, soft and silent as a shadow. The loft was dark and strange, with dim shadows where anything might be hiding. The Carver farmstead seemed a world away, bright and inviting in its cozy candlelight. By this time Uncle Moses and Aunt Susan would be yawning at their evening tasks, and Jim would be climbing the ladder to the familiar safety of the boys' bedroom.

Here every sound made George's heart hammer his bony ribs. In spite of all his care, the owner of the stable might have seen him. He might be coming out with a pitchfork.

George was tired, and the hay was fragrant, even if it was not nearly so soft as hay always looked. Below him the horses made homely, comfortable noises, snorting softly as they pulled down the hay and champed it. Gradually the almost unbearable ache of homesickness lessened. The boy slept.

Neosho, George's new home, was historically important. Here the Confederacy had established its last Missouri capital, and war had almost destroyed the town. Now it was prospering again, but it did not impress George very favorably as he slipped out of his hiding place in the early morning. Every one of his bones was aching, and his empty stomach ached even harder. And where was he to find breakfast?

He had already located his goal, Lincoln

School. Next door to it was a house that attracted him. Plain and small, it was tidy, and its dooryard was gay with flowers. George perched on a neighboring woodpile to admire the garden and nibble sunflower seeds in place of breakfast.

Then out of the brown little house trotted a black little woman who was to mean much in George's life. She meant much to him that morning, for she called him in and filled him with warm, tasty food. Then she gave him soap and water so that he could scrub off the dirt of his long walk and his hayloft bed.

The woman was Aunt Mariah Watkins, and she and Uncle Andrew were respected members of the black community. Aunt Mariah was a laundress and a nurse, and Uncle Andy an odd-jobs man, a kindly, pleasant-mannered chap. The two opened hearts and home to this smiling, soft-spoken boy, giving him for his own a curtained-off corner of their spotless one-roomed house.

Now it seemed almost fortunate that George had been a small, sickly child, unable to do heavier chores than housework. His handiness around the house gave him a good home as long as he wanted it. While doing his share of the work he learned still more about good housekeeping. He learned to cook the Watkinses' simple meals, and to do a good job of washing and ironing. He had his first taste of religion in the home, and seized upon it hungrily. Aunt Mariah gave him his first Bible, which he kept all his life, learning long passages by heart. He learned more in the Watkins home than in the school.

The school had the advantage of being near. Even during recess time George could flip over the fence and rub awhile at Aunt Mariah's tub before the big hand bell called him back. The disadvantages were the scanty education of the teacher, Stephen Frost, and the poor equipment. Seventy-five girls and boys of all ages crowded the hard benches. Knowing nothing of discipline, they wriggled, whispered and giggled, and were as hard to control as a roomful of puppies. Still, it was school. George soaked up the knowledge it offered as a sponge long dry soaks up the water in a shallow pool.

Another pleasure in George's Neosho days was the companionship of his brother, for Jim followed him there and went to school for a while. Different as the brothers were, they loved each other deeply. In one trait they were alike: both had a rollicking sense of humor. They romped together like bear cubs, and both liked to recite funny "pieces," with all the dramatic gestures then popular.

Soon, however, Jim left school and took up the plasterer's trade, which gave him a chance to travel about. Soon, too, George had taken all the

knowledge Lincoln School could give him, and
wanted to go where he could find more. Besides,
he was eager to get away from this teacher. Stephen Frost was ashamed of his race, and his
shame hurt George. Throughout his life he believed that God would not have made a majority
of the world's people different if He did not think
different skins good.

It was this belief that helped George decide to
go to Kansas. He had heard that it was a state
where a man could prove what was under his
skin, whether it was red, black or white.

Missouri, where George was born, was rich
with farmlands and forests, and its background
was as rich as its soil. Settled early, it had been
ruled by Spain and France, and sought by En-
gland. Kansas was as unlike it as a next-door
neighbor could be, but had qualities as fine. It
stood for bold adventure. It stood for freedom.
It stood for the equality of men—and later for
women's equality with men, also.

It seemed fortunate that George Carver spent
his first years in the more settled Missouri community, with its older tradition, and his later boyhood in the younger state. Kansas was a good
place for youth to try its wings.

But it was sixty miles from Neosho, and that
was a long way for a boy with no money. Luckily,
Neosho friends were moving to Fort Scott,

Kansas, and they invited George to ride with them, in their wagonload of household goods. Still undersized, George perched on a chair that topped the load, rocking comically to make the tired family laugh. Whenever the wagon stopped for a meal by the wayside, he hopped out and helped build the fire and cook.

Fort Scott proved to be a thriving little city about forty years old, a center for cattlemen from all over the Midwest. Wilder House, the hotel facing its town square, lodged most of the travelers, as it had done in stagecoach days.

At that hotel George asked for a job. Washwomen were scarce in pioneer country, so George announced that he was a washwoman. He never bothered to divide work into pigeonholes, one marked "Men" and another "Women." He believed that all kinds of work were good for all kinds of people. So this boy in his early teens, still spindly and stammering, set up a hand laundry at the hotel, earned his living there after school hours, and slept on a cot on the back porch.

School! To George the Fort School was grand beyond his dreams. Up to this time he had known only the outside of the country school near Diamond Grove, and the inside of the one-roomed Lincoln School.

At once he began making discoveries about his

schoolmates, most of whom were white. He found that they, like almost everyone else he met, only half saw, heard or smelled the world around them. They walked right over interesting plants, pebbles and bugs without knowing they were there. They looked straight at flowers or forests without seeing them. They did not seem to care how things were made, or why.

They were not half so interested in reading and spelling as George was, either. He enjoyed their surprise when he recited well in these subjects.

Yet his schoolmates knew things which he had never been taught. With only the skimpiest blackboards and slates in the Neosho school, George had not learned to write well. As for history, geography and arithmetic, they were mysteries to him, for Stephen Frost had not been able to teach them. When it came time to recite in those subjects, George made himself smaller in his half of the fine double seat, so that the teacher would not call on him. When the lessons were about strange places, times and people, George listened, wide-eyed, but in arithmetic class his mind wandered.

He looked out at the mulberry trees and wondered why they couldn't be made to bear fruit with more pulp and fewer seeds. He stared at the teacher's lace collar and planned how to crochet a prettier one for her. Often when she called on him to do a problem, he led her away from the dangerous subject by eagerly asking a question about something else. In his three years in that school he learned no arithmetic.

During that time he earned his way by cooking as well as washing. He became such a good cook that his yeast bread and salt-rising, his rolls and biscuits, took prizes at the fairs.

As a side line he was teaching himself music. A Fort Scott man who had heard him singing urged him to have his high tenor voice trained. But George had always wanted to play an instrument, from the time when he was little and made cornstalk fiddles. As soon as he could save enough money, he bought an accordion, with bells attached for accent. He was soon able to play it, though poorly.

Throughout these years, also, he was polishing up his laundering ability while he polished off clothes for his customers. Aunt Mariah had taught him to wash clean and iron neatly. Now he had a teacher even more expert, another motherly woman, of just as remarkable character and personality. This was "Aunt Lucy" Seymour.

Aunt Lucy came from Virginia, and did not let anyone forget it. She valued breeding and manners, and forbade her nephews and nieces to play with common children. She was as much impressed as Aunt Mariah by this gangling boy in his neat, shabby clothes, with his polite, proper talk. She also took him into her home, where he earned his keep by helping with fine laundry.

That was the day of hard shirt fronts for men, with separate hard cuffs and collars, which were starched and ironed to look and feel like white china. It was the day of fussy dresses, with flounces, ruffles, pleats, tucks, puffs and embroidery all on one dress, as if there were a law against leaving any plain cloth showing. Ironing such a dress took a half-day's hard labor, and great skill. The boy was soon doing work as perfect as Aunt Lucy's. If she could do it, he could do it, too.

Aunt Lucy also continued Aunt Mariah's training in religion, and in living nicely, even in a humble house. Hers was a friendly home. Uncle Seymour was as kind as she, and much more easygoing. All week he would put off hauling wood he had promised a customer, and then would have to hitch up and do it on Sunday, to Aunt Lucy's grim disapproval.

During his life in Fort Scott, George made a few journeys. When the railway was being extended to far-off, fabulous Denver, he applied for work on a construction gang. The foreman hired him, though he looked dubiously at George's slight frame, lengthening but not broadening in his late teens. For one summer George worked as cook's helper in a camp in the desert, then pressed on westward and cooked for a while on a ranch. He is said to have gone into the Southwest with migrant fruit pickers. The New Mexico vegetation charmed him, and he made sketches of the yucca, with its bristling spears and waxen bloom. Much though he may have enjoyed the brief stay in the desert, he always preferred the fertile prairies of Kansas.

It was the sight of a lynching, probably the only one in Fort Scott's history, that ended George's stay in the little city. The sensitive youth firmly believed in the dignity of all human beings, and the awful sights and sounds of that day drove him away forever.

Fortunately, the Seymours also were moving, and they welcomed his company. It was also fortunate that they were going to Minneapolis, Kansas, a place which offered further schooling for George.

Minneapolis was a clean little Central Kansas town, in the rich Solomon River Valley. Young Carver delighted in the farms around it, luxuriant with corn, rye, broomcorn and the winter wheat which the Mennonites had recently brought from Russia. The river was fringed with forest trees, and the town, about twenty years old, already had shade along its streets and around its houses of log, frame and sandstone. The Forty-Niners had followed the Solomon River to California, but the farmers who came to the Valley a few years later gained more gold per man than the gold seekers.

Here the Seymours settled in Poverty Gulch, in a poor little house of vertical boards without weatherstripping, kept spotless, like all Aunt Lucy's houses. She soon had more laundry than she could handle. Minneapolis, with a population of fifteen hundred, was the county seat. The stores, with horses lining the long hitching racks before them, were full of young clerks who wore boiled shirts and could pay to have them laundered. The many comfortable houses and the few grand ones with towers and cupolas were also filled with eager customers.

So young Carver set up business for himself. Like the Seymours, he settled in Poverty Gulch, a ravine below the business street, crossed by a high boardwalk like a footbridge. Though one end of his two-room shack of cottonwood slabs was crowded with washtubs, stove and ironing board, he kept the other end homelike as well as clean. Wherever he lived, he had blossoming plants, wild flowers in their season and collections of stones and last year's birds' nests. His hard bed was always neatly made up, with clean sheets and a fancy pillow case. In the shack in Poverty Gulch, he also painted pictures on the flimsy walls.

The few blacks in town were scattered among the whites, attending the white school and white churches. George Carver went to the Presbyterian Church, and to the big, square, four-roomed schoolhouse a block up from the main street. It had four teachers and a principal, and one of its rooms was the high school. Going to so advanced a school was to George like going to Paradise.

At first Minneapolis took little notice of the youth, now grown remarkably tall and thin. Soon, however, he was amazing his teachers by a knowledge of natural science beyond their own.

With so few rooms, classes reciting and classes studying could not be kept separate, so it was the rule that those who were studying should pay no attention to those who were reciting. For George the teachers made an exception. His recitations were so interesting and instructive that the other pupils were allowed to close their books and listen to him.

Minneapolis soon found that the newcomer was musical as well as clever. In spite of a slow start, he had not given up the accordion, but had mastered it by patient practice. Soon he was invited to lead the school marches with its stirring music. Someone had given him a minister's long coat, and he made an amusing picture playing and marching zestfully at the head of the student body, the skirts of the stately coat flapping round his lanky legs. People laughed at the sight, but they liked George.

Some of his laundry customers enjoyed his music, too. The lively young store clerks and courthouse employees found little entertainment in the small town. Bringing their laundry and calling for it gave them an opportunity to pass a pleasant hour with George Carver. Sometimes they all sang together, making a stylish group in their stiff collars, fat satin ties and derby hats, while George accompanied them on accordion and mouth organ at the same time. Sometimes he sang solos, ''Buffalo Gals'' and other popular songs of the day. Sometimes they coaxed him to recite funny ''pieces.''

He had so much business that it often kept him from school. Then he would put his books up over tubs and ironing board and study while he worked. His teachers would invite him to come to their homes and recite his lessons in the evening, and when his washings kept him too busy to go to them, they would come down to Poverty Gulch and hear his recitations while he worked.

Part of the time he also took care of the Presbyterian meetinghouse. One of his friends often scolded him for doing so much. What did he want all that book-learning for, anyway? she used to ask. With his bad throat and his frequent, heavy colds, he should not work so hard. And he didn't need any more schooling, for he already knew more than was good for him.

George only laughed at her objections. "I need to know all there is to know. You wait and see. Someday you'll be reading my name in the papers."

Mrs. Saunders laughed with him at his joking boast, but she was not satisfied. At least, she said, he needn't run to the church every time its doors were opened, as if it couldn't hold a meeting without him. But George had a streak of pure stubbornness, and he was stubborn about church. To him it was the House of God. Nothing could make him give up God. "And nothing will ever make me give up the church," he said obstinately.

Mrs. Saunders fretted also over his lack of social life. He was friendly with the other young blacks, but he could not spare time for play. His hope of having his own school may have grown dim, but his will to learn all there was to learn burned brighter than ever.

He did find time to see every point of interest around Minneapolis. In order to visit Rock City, beyond the Solomon River, he drove someone's ox team out there to water. He was so impressed by what he saw that he let the oxen run away and came near getting into trouble.

Those rocks! Some were like badly weathered croquet balls, ten feet high, others like giant hornet nests. How had they been shaped? And how had they come to this prairie, where no other rocks could be seen? Had they been rolled and tossed by the glaciers George had read about?

For several years George stayed in Minneapolis, completing all the high-school courses available. At that time, early in the eighteen-eighties, few white boys and girls went further than high school. Still fewer blacks went so far, even of those who were not, like George, orphaned, penniless and sickly. Everyone thought he should be both proud and satisfied with his high school diploma.

But George had college in his dreams, and he was one who made his dreams come true. "If anyone can do it, I can." He had hunted up a college to which he hoped his sketchy schooling might admit him. It was a Kansas institution, with attractive courses, and with a small enough enrollment so that it was likely to be lenient in its requirements. To this college, Highland, he sent his record of school work and grades.

Anxiously he awaited its reply. Working at his tubs, sweeping the church, attending the last of his high-school classes, he was tense with anxiety. Highland might easily reply, "Sorry, but you have not had enough mathematics—you have not had enough parsing and diagramming—you have simply Not Had Enough.'' And then what would George do?

At last the postmaster thrust through the post-office window the long awaited envelope, addressed in the large, flowing penmanship of the time. Even George's deft hands must have fumbled as he drew out the letter. Then his world turned pink with joy. President Duncan Brown wrote that he was welcome in Highland University. Moreover, he offered him a special scholarship because of his good grades.

That summer George followed a Minneapolis friend and classmate, Chester Rarig, to Kansas City. Chester had opened a business school in the booming town, and George felt that typing would help him in college and afterward. Somewhere along the line he had learned to play the organ, and he gave Chester Rarig organ lessons in exchange for business instruction.

By teaching music and working as typist in the Union Depot while studying stenography, he earned enough to go back to Diamond Grove for a visit before college opened in the fall. He would see the Carvers, but not his brother. Jim had died of smallpox in Fayetteville, Arkansas.

The visit to the Carvers was a triumph. They could not stop exclaiming over his six feet of height and his good looks, or fussing over his stoop-shouldered thinness. Everyone was astonished at his voice. It was still high and soft, and when he sang with the congregation in church, people turned their heads to locate the clear, sweet tenor with its unusual range.

But to Diamond Grove the most astounding thing about George was his plan for going to college. He enjoyed their amazement. He himself was so overcome by joyful wonder that he could not keep his voice steady when he talked of the dream so soon to come true.

George asked to sleep, during his visit, in his mother's old cabin, near the Carver house. There he spent busy hours, more happy than sad, cleaning out the rubbish that had gathered in twenty years, and decking the scrubbed interior with flowers and vines.

At night he lay long awake, with moonlight streaming between unchinked logs and stretching a broad mellow bar through the open door. Whippoorwills called, and mockingbirds scolded melodiously. Breezes cooled the warm cabin, and sighed pleasantly in the elms and walnuts high above the roof. Here in the place where he was born he felt nearer his mother than ever before.

When he left the Carvers, Aunt Susan gave him his mother's spinning wheel. To the end of his days he kept it with him, moving the great cumbersome thing from one place to another. Some say that the Carvers also gave him the lamp which had cost him a thrashing when he carried it out to the barn long before.

Finally, with pockets emptied, he set out to go to his life's high goal, college. The empty pockets did not troubled him. With the promised scholarship to help with his tuition and with clothes always needing a laundryman and empty stomachs demanding a cook, the world was his.

The little town of Highland looked beautiful to George when he stepped off the train. The university campus seemed a gateway to glory. There he would give all he had, and in return Highland would give him—But what would it not give him?

With shy dignity he passed through the door of the brick administration building and walked softly into the president's office. He stood politely silent before the desk until the president looked up. Then George smiled, a smile remarkably warm and glowing for so young a man. Dr. Duncan stared at him inquiringly.

"I am a new student," the young man said in a high, gentle voice. "I am George Carver."

The president's eyes widened. Perhaps his surprise made him speak before he had time to soften his words.

"But we don't take niggers here," he said.

3

Inching Along

IN ALL HIS TWENTY-ODD YEARS George Carver had been able to overcome every hardship. This was different. It was the blackest moment of his life when Dr. Duncan lifted amazed eyes and said, "But we don't take niggers here."

George Carver turned and stumbled from the office, from the building, from the campus.

He had always known that his fight for a college education would be a stiff one, but he had never doubted the outcome. He had been patient. He had been industrious. He had worked when tired and sick. Then he had confidently taken the next step. And that next step had brought him up against a stone wall that had no way over, or through, or around.

The wall had not only stopped him; it had bruised and broken him. As he stumbled away from Highland University he began to wonder

44

whether he had not been mistaken about himself and his powers. He began to wonder if the color of his skin did, after all, reach through and taint his brain. He began to feel the unsureness which makes life unbearable. He actually asked himself, Am I a human being? George Carver was beaten.

More than anything else, he wanted to get so far away that he need never again see the mocking walls of the college, nor hear its name. But his pockets were empty. He must stay here where he had been shamed till he could earn enough to escape. It was a time which left lifelong scars on George Carver's spirit.

Yet even that bitter season was not without friendship. Some townspeople heard what had happened, and offered the tall, quiet young man work. One such family were the Beelers, who had a fruit farm near Highland. They took George into their home as a helper. They invited him to church, and to church socials.

No matter how deeply he was hurt, George Carver never wanted to hurt anyone. Rather than wound friends, he accepted their invitations. He even took his accordion and mouth organ to the socials, and charmed everyone with his playing, singing and reciting. Yet with all the kindnesses the Beelers and the church could offer him, George seized his first chance to get away from

Highland. That chance came through Frank
Beeler.

Western Kansas had been opened to homesteaders in 1878. Now there was a new wave of
migration to the Great American Desert, as
Kansas prairies were called. Frank Beeler had
taken up land there and founded a town which
bore his name. Anything would grow in that vir-
gin soil, he said—if it had water. His enthusiasm
led George to follow him there.

Taking up a hundred and sixty acres two miles
south of town, he built a house and put in his first
crops. While he waited for harvest, he worked on
the Gregg-Seeley Stock Ranch adjoining his
homestead, helping Mr. Seeley erect farm buildings. These were made of sod, for there were
miles of it for the cutting, and no other building
material in reach.

The unbroken prairie soil was cut in long strips
with the plow, and the strips cut crosswise into
huge bricks. They held together firmly, for the
roots of the prairie grasses had woven a strong
web through the earth. These giant bricks were
laid up in walls, logs and poles placed across, and
sod spread on the logs and poles, to form a flat
roof.

Soddies had disadvantages. If the roofs were
not patched continually, it rained indoors when-

ever it rained outdoors. Because dirt floors and walls were inclined to be dirty, some settlers lined the walls with muslin; but rattlesnakes often worked their way between the sod bricks, and rattled away fearfully behind the muslin.

George Carver whitewashed his walls instead of lining them. When he made his first soddies he was a pupil, but he soon became a teacher. Studying out new ways to cut the turf clean and straight, he learned to put up the smoothest, solidest houses in the region. As always, he was doing common things uncommonly well.

The thick walls and roof kept the soddies cool under blazing summer suns and warm against freezing winter winds. When the turf blossomed in spring, George Carver had a flower garden on his roof; and in winter his cabin was a greenhouse. Neighbors used to come in out of a blizzard that had frozen their eyelashes, and find his deep-silled windows bright with blossoming plants.

The house was homelike, with fancy pillow-cases George Carver had made, and "throws" for the shelves, of bolting cloth or velvet, painted with wild roses, poppies, wheat. He had neat displays of his usual collections, too, minerals, Indian relics, and stones which he had polished in a way he had worked out. His neighbors marveled at the neat efficiency of everything he did. They even listened when he told them gravely that there was "treasure under the ground here." He had found that when the land was shaped like a low dome, it paid to find out what was inside. Sure enough, the Beeler oil field was later discovered there.

In Ness County George Carver was among friends from the first, for many of the Beelers had settled there. Whenever he went to the post office, run by Elmer Beeler, he would sit down to the organ in the Beelers' living quarters, for he could never pass a musical instrument without getting a tune out of it. The young girl who helped in the post office, Margaret Livingood, noticed that he often played the same tune, "inching along like a poor inchworm." He still felt like a worm, and one that had been stepped on by a merciless foot.

All the townspeople and homesteaders liked him. Capable in his work, friendly and interesting, he was also personally neat and pleasing. His shabby clothes were clean and brushed, his close-cropped hair was well combed, and his white celluloid collar was finished with a broad cravat, ready tied, as was the style.

He never pushed himself. Anyone who wanted George Carver had to pull him. The one place he went rain or shine and without having to be coaxed was to church, which was held in the schoolhouse. When blizzards kept the organist away, George Carver spread his amazingly long fingers on the keyboard and played any hymn that was called for. He knew them all.

The country was unlike any George Carver had ever known. Flat prairie—"perara," the people called it—stretched unbroken to the skyline. Its principal inhabitants were lazily sailing buzzards, crows, rattlesnakes, and prairie dogs sitting erect and chattering. The only trees were cottonwoods, which seemed to walk in processions along the few small streams, offering shade from the blistering sun. The newness of the broad landscape had given George Carver a measure of release from his pain and hopelessness.

As his spirit revived enough so that he felt able to face the world again, he came to doubt whether this was the place for him. He had always dreamed of helping his people. Here there were few black homesteaders, and he could find no way to help the few. And what about his dream of knowing everything in this great, wonderful world? He could not make that dream come true in Ness County. Besides, he did not want to invest his life in a land of terrible blizzards, parching droughts, and summer winds that shriveled the brave young corn in a single day of blazing fury. George Carver still had to put his whole self into his work. So his work must be something that mattered to him, even if nobody else cared about it.

"You can always make what you want out of what you have." What did he have by this time? The same sickliness with which he had set out from the Carver farm years ago; the same mastery of the skills of a farm home, greatly developed by use; the same love of flowers and the green thumb to make them flourish; and, added to these, a half-finished education.

Then why not take these assets to a milder climate and work toward making a greenhouse of his own? Why not produce loveliness which could make his living while he enjoyed it? His color ought not to stand in the way of his growing flowers.

So George Carver mortgaged his homestead for enough money to tide him over, and turned eastward. He was lowering his aim. Simply to earn a living was a small ambition compared with his childhood dream of service.

Eastward and northward he pushed, toward the heart of Iowa. Sometimes he saw the country as a great green saucer, its turned-up edge decorated with tidy toy farmsteads, complete with planted fields, windmills, red-painted barns and white-painted houses. The vast saucer was trimmed with smooth circles: velvety green rounds that were knolls high with corn and smaller rounds made by green trees. The round bowl of the blue sky, with snowy round puffs of cloud, was neatly turned over the saucer to keep it safe and clean. It was beautiful. Here George Carver could put down roots.

The first Iowa town where he stayed was Winterset. For five terrible years it had been attacked by armies of grasshoppers and almost destroyed, but by the time George Carver arrived, it had recovered. George's eye was taken by the slow-growing hard maples which made a wall of beauty around its substantial courthouse. He also liked the cheap living which Winterset offered, with corn fifteen cents a bushel and eggs eight cents a dozen. He decided to find a job there.

At the Schultz Hotel, on one of the main corners, he overheard the proprietor complaining that he had lost his cook. George offered his services, and the proprietor gave him a trial. Not only was he delighted with the young man's cookery, but also with his economy. He had never had a cook who made so little money go so far.

Here George found a priceless possession: spare time. There was never time enough for the fascinating things he found to do, so he would rather have wasted a pound of butter than an hour. Whenever he was free from his hotel work he tramped through the woods around the town, and along the streams with their wooded banks and sunny clearings. Intent on the treasures he was finding, he often failed to see the farmers, but when they laughingly roused him, he was always shyly friendly.

One farm boy, Clyde Robbins, met him when he was gathering wild hops in the Robbins woodlot. George was carrying a basket, and had a stick slipped across his back and under his arms. His posture had always been poor, and he had heard that a stick so held would straighten the spine. He could not waste time exercising, so he was delighted with an exercise that fitted in with the things he wanted to do.

Like everyone else, Clyde Robbins was astonished at the young man's high, soft voice when he spoke. That day it was hoarse, and George explained that his colds always lodged in his throat.

"Say, listen!" Clyde cried boyishly. "You come along home with me, and Mother will cure your throat in no time."

Thus started another of George Carver's many lifelong friendships. Mrs. Robbins was a lively, independent little lady, and her hands fairly itched to help this homeless boy. She had seen him before, when he came quietly into the Baptist church and sat down at the far end of her pew. Mrs. Robbins had moved the length of the seat to share her hymnbook with him.

Now she clucked over his swollen throat with the relish of a born nurse when she meets a challenging case. She used fluid extract of aconite, a risky drug, she said, but a good remedy in skilled hands.

George was interested, for he knew aconite came from the monkshood family. He spread out the herbs and roots he had gathered that day, and the two found common ground in their knowledge of medicinal plants.

Mrs. Robbins urged him to spend a week at her house, so that she could clear up the ugly throat with a thorough course of treatment. Because of his hotel job he could not accept the invitation, but he came each day, his throat was healed for that time, and he became a welcome friend in the Robbins home.

Mrs. Robbins was not the only one who had noticed the stranger and his voice in church. At the end of the service a fine-appearing gentleman introduced himself as Dr. Milholland. His wife, the choir director, he said, had admired George's singing. Later the doctor hunted him up at

Schultz Hotel and invited him to their home. Mrs. Milholland wanted to talk to him about music and art.

George was both frightened and excited. He washed his shirt and ironed it with professional care. Then he washed and ironed his trousers and his one coat. In his buttonhole he stuck the flower which was to become his trademark. Only then did he feel properly dressed for the occasion.

The Milholland house was elegant in the style of the eighteen-eighties, with thick carpets, rich wallpapers, carved furniture, starched lace curtains and heavy draperies. But the full bookcases and the big square piano were what set George's pulses hammering.

Mrs. Milholland was as kind as she was musical. Her caller's sensitive nature was written on his fine face, and she had already heard that he would not accept the smallest favor unless he could repay it. So, after she had played for him and he for her, she told him of her struggles with painting and asked help.

An ardent gardener, she had tried to capture on canvas the beauty of her garden, but with little success. She had heard about George's flower paintings on the walls of his hotel room. Would he look at her attempts and tell her what was wrong?

In addition to music and education, Carver's talents and passions as a young man included painting. For several years he harbored a dream of making art his life's work.

At his eager consent, she got out her equipment and half-finished pictures. George's eyes lighted with pleasure at sight of her expensive paints, and with horror at the state of her palettes and costly camel's-hair brushes.

"Oh, my, my, my!" he whispered in gentle distress, "such brushes, such brushes! If you wash them well with laundry soap after each using they will last twice as long. And please let me clean your palette for you, Mrs. Milholland. Tk, tk! A pity to waste all that beautiful paint, but it is useless when it dries."

Once he had the fine wood clean and smooth, he showed her how to squeeze out the colors she needed in orderly array, neither too much nor too little. Thus she could work better as well as save precious paint, he explained mildly.

Dr. Milholland doubtless smiled behind his mustache at the success of his wife's friendly scheme. For after George Carver showed her some of the ways he had worked out for painting flowers, she asked whether he would be willing to give her painting lessons in exchange for piano lessons from her. He had a pianist's hands, she said, long, strong fingers with delicately squared tips.

Would he be willing? Eagerly George Carver seized the opportunity.

He went often to the Milholland house and—characteristically—gave as much as he received. He not only helped Mrs. Milholland with her painting, but worked in her garden and made it increasingly beautiful. In return, he used her piano and her able instruction, and spent long hours in the sunny bay window, reading and studying the Milhollands' books.

As the months passed, the Milhollands often puzzled about the young man lost in the wonders of the printed page. Surely he did not mean to continue as hotel cook. Surely with his clear mind and many gifts, he should go on to college.

George Carver had hidden the Highland experience deep in his sore heart. Now he told these new friends what had made him so unsure, so hopeless. It was not the disappointment of missing college, he explained, so much as the horror of seeing himself contemptible in another person's eyes. He felt that it had killed in him something that could never grow again. He confessed that he did not believe he could live through another shock so bitter.

The Milhollands had an answer to his fears. Only a few miles away, in Indianola, was a small school, Simpson College. Here George need not fear another wound. When he remained doubtful, his friends told him more. Some thirty years earlier, Mathew Simpson, a Methodist bishop, had used all his savings to start the college. Like his personal friend, Abraham Lincoln, he believed in the equality of all men, and his school stood for that belief.

Hearing this, George Carver decided to give college one more try. This time he sent in no application. A person's writing did not show the color of his skin, but if he applied in person, there could be no mistake.

He walked the intervening twenty-five miles, through the softly rounded green landscapes which the painter Grant Wood later made famous, and came to Indianola. It was another typical Iowa town, with the added charm of being built around a college and somewhat shaped by its ideas and ideals.

George Carver was not a dramatic figure as he tramped into town. He was tall, thin, stooped, shabby. He had a diffident gait, knees bending and feet dragging slightly. It was the walk of a boy who had been the smallest and weakest in his group. It was the walk of a youth who had learned that he was a member of a despised race. It was the walk of a man who had too many interesting things before him to waste time by carrying a chip on his shoulder.

If George Carver did not look dramatic, he had plenty of drama within as he forced himself to cross the small campus and enter the president's office. In his heart drums were beating. He would try this once more.

It seemed to him that the success of his whole life hung on his acceptance or rejection by President Holmes of Simpson College, on that fourth day of September, 1890.

4

When You Do the Common Things Uncommonly Well

I OFTEN SHUDDER to think what would have happened if Simpson had not given me a chance." So George Carver wrote long afterward to a friend on the faculty of that college.

When he laid on the desk records that fluttered in his shaking hands, President Holmes studied the papers courteously and said that Simpson would gladly enroll George. The victory was won.

George must think next of his bread and butter. He asked whether Indianola needed another good laundry. Yes, Dr. Holmes said, and he would announce in assembly that Mr. George Carver, a new student, was opening a hand laundry and would welcome patronage.

Dizzy with joy, George Carver went to hunt a place for his bed, stove and wash tubs. The owner of an empty woodshed near the campus gave him the use of it. He had only ten cents left, so he bought tubs, irons, washboard on credit, though he hated debt. When the washings began to pour in he could quickly pay for the simple equipment.

He refused to ask credit for food. The dime bought five cents worth of suet and five cents worth of corn meal. He could live on these till he earned money to buy more.

Unfortunately, the kind president was absent-minded, and George Carver listened in vain for the promised announcement. Though prices were only a fraction of today's, George had eaten his dime's worth of food in two weeks.

His friends, luckily, had not forgotten him. Mrs. Milholland had asked Mrs. Liston, of Indianola, to look out for him. Mrs. Liston visited his laundry, learned what had happened, and went to the president. He remorsefully made the over-due announcement, the washings began to come in, and George Carver ate again. He had plenty of work, for everyone in town was interested. George Carver was Simpson's first black student, and townspeople, teachers and schoolmates soon found him both surprising and interesting.

The first surprise was his announcement that he meant to study art. Most of his subjects would be of preparatory grade, to fill in the gaps in his early schooling. That was not unusual at Simpson, where many students came from rural schools without standardized courses. Mr. Carver's choices of arithmetic, grammar, etymology and essay were praiseworthy, but his wish for art was utterly impractical.

Here George Carver's stubbornness showed itself. He did not dutifully give up his plan.

He had a class in the science hall, and his heart swelled with joy whenever he entered that new building, which had cost the large sum of twenty thousand dollars. The lofty arched windows thrilled the new student. The long work tables, the beakers and retorts, the choking chemical smells excited him. Here a willing student could probe the mysteries of the marvelous world. But George Carver did not stop with the laboratories. Doggedly determined, he climbed the great winding stair to the top floor and the art department.

Looking through the open doors of the studio, he gulped air intoxicating with charcoal dust, oil paint and turpentine. Ever since the day when he saw his first oil painting and tried to copy it with turkey-feather brushes and berry-juice paint, he had been plodding toward this mountain peak. Then and there he knew that painting was what he loved best of anything on earth.

On every wall hung pictures in oil, pastel,

watercolor. Through the broad room were scattered plaster casts of Greek statues. Here stood a cabinet of hand-painted china and yonder six or eight easels where students were drawing or painting. George Carver's eyes devoured the delight and promise of that room.

Questioningly the teacher moved toward the enraptured young man. Miss Etta Budd was fresh from college, but she had dignity and poise. She nearly lost the poise when the new freshman said he had come to enroll in art. Art was not practical, she urged, glancing at his shabby suit and thin wrists.

George Carver stood his ground. He would be able to pay the extra fees, he told her eagerly. His laundry would provide the needed money. His glowing eagerness defeated Miss Budd. She enrolled George Carver in Simpson's art courses.

The next year and a half was a time of pure happiness for George. The campus was kind to him. The boys brought him all their washing, and their mending, besides, since George was an expert at mending and patching. He was welcomed into a literary society, which met in a high-shouldered upper room in the chapel building. He pleased his fellow members by decking the bare meeting place with charming arrangements of vines and wild flowers.

Simpson students would look strangely mature to coming generations. The girls wore high collars, skirts to their toes, sleeves to their wrists, and hair in Psyche knots and curled bangs. Many of the boys cherished mustaches. Nevertheless, old copies of the *Simp*, as the campus paper was nicknamed, show that both boys and girls were much like students today. Though George Carver had more youthful fun with them than he had ever known before, he behaved with such dignity that he did not offend even those who had been doubtful about having a black student among the white ones.

He was soon famous for his humor, for the beauty of his speech, for his funny "pieces," and for his musical gifts. He was noted also for fancy penmanship, then a branch of art and an accomplishment to be proud of. His writing looked as if engraved, with hairlike lines going up and heavy black ones coming down, and with a maze of loops and curls. His spread-winged doves were popular, each drawn with a single stroke of his steel pen.

Off the campus, he found his warmest welcome in the Liston house, a comfortably rambling place, set in shady lawns and gardens. Here George left his mark by bringing the flowers to new beauty. Here also he could often be found bent over a book in the square bay window.

All his teachers were friendly, but Miss Etta Budd was the most interested and understanding. Besides heading Simpson's art department, she assisted in chemistry, physics and mathematics. Learning of George's weakness in arithmetic, she helped him with it.

She was trained in another subject, second only to art in George Carver's affection, and that was botany. Her father was professor of Horticulture in State College at Ames, Iowa. After a lifelong contact with the science of plants, Etta Budd had taken the usual college course in botany. She gave George Carver his first scientific answers to the questions he had always asked, and for which he had worked out his own partial explanations. Hungrily he seized all she could give him. When, for example, she said that a plant's food could affect the color of its bloom, her pupil experimented, and astonished her by bringing her a blue geranium.

She often saw him going out at dawn with his tin botanical case. He brought new specimens to class, and he brought house plants which he had started from slips, and shyly asked if he might keep them in the sunny studio. He continued to bring them, and they continued to grow, until they filled a table in the hall window outside the studio entrance.

One day he brought in something entirely different: a bulging pillowcase. While Miss Budd stared amazedly, he emptied out on her desk, not plants, pebbles nor Indian arrowheads, but dozens of patterns of lace, knitted or crocheted.

"Why, George, where did you get these?"

"I made them."

"But—what for?" she asked in surprise.

"For my school. I've always planned to have a school for my people. I shall teach not just book subjects, but everything that will help make their lives brighter."

Miss Budd stared from the bits of lace to her pupil's long, strong fingers.

"Girls will come to my school as well as boys," he explained. "I want to teach them cooking and sewing and even fancy work, so that they can make their homes prettier."

As winter came on, Miss Budd could not help noticing the thinness of the young man's shabby clothes, and how he stepped along, shivering, without an overcoat. She had laid aside the art fees he had paid. She added to these and bought a warm coat. First she had to plot with a neighbor to find out his size secretly, for the gift must be a surprise and the giver unknown, since George Carver was unwilling to accept anything he had not earned. After all his teacher's trouble, he did not often wear the fine overcoat, though he sometimes showed his gratitude by carrying it over his arm.

Much as Miss Budd admired her strange pupil, she was not impressed by his paintings of land-scapes and still life. It was when he helped a classmate paint roses that she realized his un-usual gift. In the field he loved best he had gen-uine talent, and flowers were that field.

He had painted a picture of his own experi-ment in grafting a cactus, and she showed it to her father, for it showed skill not only in painting but in the field of botany. It was this picture that brought a heavy sorrow to George Carver.

"George," she asked him, after her father had seen the picture, "what do you plan to do?"

He looked at her in surprise, lines of patience already marking his brow.

"I mean, what will you make your life work?"

He looked past her at the dozen of his flower studies that held places of honor in the studio. "My school—" he said—"and my painting—"

"Few artists earn a living," Miss Budd warned him.

"I can always earn a living. I've paid my own way since I was ten or twelve."

Miss Budd waved toward his plants, growing richly as if to repay the long brown hands that loved them. "You are as good at growing plants as you are at painting them," she said. "You could earn a better living that way, and be more useful as well. You could do more to help your people. George, my father and I both think you should go to Ames, Iowa State College."

It was as if her unwelcome words turned the light on a secret place where he had tried to hide the truth from himself. To leave the Simpson studio was to leave Paradise; and after the years at Ames he could see the hardships, the unkindnesses he must meet in the workaday world. His heartache rang solemnly in the words which his teacher was to remember all her life.

"Miss Budd," he said sadly, "you don't know what it is to be a colored man."

5

You Will Command the Attention of the World

WHEN IT BECAME CLEAR to George Carver that he ought to make science his career rather than painting, his heart was heavy. Yet as soon as he accepted the fact, he acted upon it. With Professor Budd's help, he arranged to enter Iowa State College.

The school was the largest and most important that he had yet attended. Its campus was large, with a deep ravine, a brook, a lake, and grassy flats rolling into gentle heights and hollows. All this was shaded by a hundred varieties of fine trees.

In the newly developing science of agriculture it was ahead of its times. Its staff was to supply the United States with two future Secretaries of Agriculture, ''Tama Jim'' Wilson and ''Uncle Henry'' Wallace. Among its able faculty members

a gentle, scholarly botanist, Dr. Pammell, was
outstanding.

Even in this sizable institution, George Carver's coming roused some excitement, for he was
its first black student. But the spirit of the school
was friendly, and he was not only accepted but
welcomed. Soon it was noted that he was the
most popular man on the campus. His popularity
was apparent in the dining hall, where each of the
small tables seated eight boys and girls, and the
eights were shifted every two weeks to promote
acquaintanceship. George Carver had more invitations to join new tables than any other student
in the hall.

He always brought gaiety. In one of the meal-
time games he started, everyone must ask for
food under its scientific name. ''Please pass the
sodium chloride,'' meant ''Please pass the salt.''
''Another helping of solanum tuberosum,
please,'' would bring the potatoes. No scientific
name, no food. The table was always in a gale of
laughter.

George Carver was not one of the campus
pranksters who climbed the tallest college smoke-
stack and painted the class numerals on it, but he
did enjoy the fun and celebrate it in a long class
poem he was asked to write for the *Bomb*, the
school yearbook.

His studies took more time than they would have if his early schooling had been more regular. In spite of Miss Budd's help, he was still shaky in mathematics. For a while it looked as it he would fail at Iowa State for lack of that one subject. But George Carver could not be beaten by arithmetic, dull though he found it. With the help of a teacher as determined as he, he overcame the enemy and passed the course.

He was as busy outside school hours as inside. Learning of his artistic skill, Dr. Pammell asked him to make drawings for scientific bulletins. Soon he was making microscopic pictures of plant diseases for the Iowa Agricultural Society, his work attracting attention by its faithful detail.

He worked also in the campus greenhouse. Seaman Knapp, small son of a professor, often went there to get flowers for his mother, and to visit the tall young man. With childish pride he took playmates along and showed off his friendship with this remarkable person. George Carver let the little boys help him transplant seedlings, and they crammed plants into pots with clumsy zeal. Gently disapproving, George Carver showed them how to handle each plant as tenderly as if it were a baby.

During those years at Ames, George did not have to run a laundry. He did make and peddle lye hominy to bring in a little cash. He also served as masseur for the school athletes, for he already had a thorough knowledge of the human body, and his hands were powerful.

He was active in the Y.M.C.A., and served on a student team that visited the surrounding towns, speaking and singing. His voice remained as notable as his hands. When people first heard George Carver speak, they were always surprised and amused. When they first heard him sing, they were surprised and delighted. At Ames he had vocal training which helped bring his once paralyzed throat under control. His speaking voice always retained a weird quality, but he sang so well in a college quartet that he was offered a scholarship in a Boston school of music.

He joined the Welch Eclectic, one of the literary societies, and according to the *Zenith*, campus paper, he took part in most of the meetings. ''Mr. Carver gave a reading depicting an evening on the farm.'' Mr. Carver was asked for ''something funny,'' and responded with ''a humorous reading,'' and so on.

As at Simpson, he decorated the clubroom. He also trimmed the tables for the State Agricultural Society banquet: ''George Washington Carver decorated the hall with vines and autumn leaves, making it a thing of beauty." The *Zenith* also comments that "the only refreshing spots on the campus are the flower beds. . . . kept in a fine condition by Mr. Carver." And in the *Bomb*, among the teasing and often belittling descriptions of other students, this caption accompanies his name: "Doctor—whom not even critics criticize."

It was almost impossible to find time for his painting, but he managed to. He took more lessons from Miss Budd. He went back to Simpson for a summer term of art, and would have returned for another, if the school physician had not forbidden him. Several of his flower paintings were accepted and hung in the art exhibit of the Chicago World's Fair in 1893. The child of the Ozarks, dabbing homemade paint on tin and pasteboard with feather brushes, had come a long way.

At last, in 1894, he reached the lofty peak of graduation and his Bachelor of Science degree. Moreover, he was at once made a member of the college staff, the first black to serve on the faculty of Iowa State.

The next two years increased his busy happiness. He was earning his Master of Science degree while working as station assistant in the botany section of the staff. Often, too, he traveled through the state, giving talks on agricultural subjects.

With all his tasks, he found time for friendship. In undergraduate days, friends in classes and on the staff gave him a surprise party. Getting him out of the way by a trick, they refurnished his bare room for him. After graduation he enjoyed more of the social life of the campus. A group of staff members held social evenings, with games and light refreshments, the popular chafing-dish dainties, or cocoa and cookies. George Carver, with his humorous readings and music, was always in great demand.

He valued these friends, as they valued him. He was always giving them things he had painted, carved or crocheted, in thanks for their kindnesses. Perhaps it was a fault in him that he hated to accept favors without a return. All his life his friends found that anything they did for him must be wrapped up in laughter and tied with a big bowknot of fun.

Mrs. Stebbins, wife of the campus carpenter and superintendent of buildings, for example, worried because the young teacher's shoes were thin and he had no overshoes. Iowa weather was sometimes dreamlike, but it was often wet and chill. Damp feet still gave George Carver severe sore throat. So the motherly Mrs. Stebbins resolved that he should have galoshes, whether he liked it or not. She wrote this jingle to go with them:

> The size we think is right, sir,
> For your "understanding" quite, sir,
> For we measure in this light, sir,
> The understanding of a MAN.

It was during these quiet, pleasant years that the six-year-old son of one of the professors began to hang around George Carver. Professor Carver took little Henry on long walks and showed him the wonders of the earth. He showed him the difference in the grasses, and their tiny blossoms, which most people never see, and he praised the child for his ability to tell the kinds apart. George Carver's praise gave Henry Wallace belief in himself and a lifelong love of the good earth. The two were still warm friends when the boy followed in his father's footsteps and became United States Secretary of Agriculture.

Though Ames held much warm friendship and satisfaction, it brought him also a new and sorrowful struggle connected with his painting. Standing at his easel, the tidy rainbow of his palette on one thumb, he was completely happy. To put his beloved flowers on canvas was supreme joy. While he lovingly laid on colors fresh

and dewy as the petals, the hours flew past unnoticed. While he was painting he was a man,
with none of the stumbling blocks which all his
life had tripped him, slowed him, bruised him.

Might Miss Budd have been mistaken about
his calling? One day he said wistfully to his
friend, Professor Wilson, that he might, after all,
serve the world best by painting for it. Well,
George Carver was gifted: Professor Wilson
thought him the finest painter in Iowa. But
George was gifted as remarkably in agricultural
science. And by making science his life work, he
said gravely, George Carver could do more to
serve his people than he could possibly do
through painting.

Again George Carver was convinced against
his will. Again he chose science. For a whole year
he kept his paints and brushes locked away out of
his sight. So keen was his sense of loss that his
heart ached with physical pain. Yet the will of
God was law to him and he believed that God has
spoken to him through his wise friend.

After a time he allowed himself to paint a little,
for recreation, and the happiness of his life at
Ames was complete. His work also was increasingly pleasant. Besides having charge of the
greenhouse, he experimented in grafting and
crossing fruit trees, and made a large collection of

diseased plant specimens for the study of mycology, or plant disease. All in all, Ames was his Promised Land. A homeless wanderer, frail and often ill, he had found here home, comfort, medical care. Shy and sensitive, he had found friendship, respect, admiration. And he had found a place where he could serve the world through this fast-growing science of agriculture.

What had become of the bright dream that had filled the curly little head of Carvers' George? The dream had led him to schools in three states, had pulled him up from deep pits of discouragement. What had happened to it?

During the past few years, that dream of having a school for his people had been hidden under the work and joy of the present. He had been urged to go into the Deep South, as professor of Agriculture in a Mississippi college, but Ames was too dear a harbor to be left without long debate. The president of Iowa State and its staff were as unwilling to lose George Carver as he was unwilling to go.

Then into his earthly paradise came a bombshell which threatened to destroy all his peace and joy.

6

Make What You Want

THE BOMBSHELL WHICH EXPLODED in Professor Carver's peaceful life was a letter from Booker T. Washington.

In some ways Dr. Washington's life story was like Mr. Carver's. Born a slave without a family name, he had worked hard in the salt mines even when a young child. For him, too, the first glimpse into the world of knowledge was through a thin blue-backed speller, his most prized belonging. He, too, learned the book by heart, and with no one to teach him the letters. He, too, longed for school. He was overjoyed when some blacks started a school near his home, but his joy turned to despair, for his stepfather forbade him to attend.

Although everything seemed against him, he gained an education, and grew up with a deep love for learning and a burning wish to help his people. With that purpose he built up a school and became in the process the greatest black leader of his day, admired and respected by the white world and his own.

He was not sorry that he was black. Well as he knew the hard road his race must walk, he used to say he would have chosen it if the choice had been his. He felt that the ambitious black boy developed greater strength and determination through the hard task of overcoming the handicap of a despised heritage. He also believed that a white boy's favored race could not in the long run carry him ahead unless he had ability and worth, and that the black boy's race could not in the long run hold him back, if he had that ability and worth.

Mr. Carver well knew the story of Tuskegee Institute, Dr. Washington's school in Alabama. It had started in an old church building, with thirty pupils and one teacher, Mr. Washington. When the school was offered a fine stretch of rolling ground near the town for five hundred dollars, the treasurer of Hampton Institute, an older black school, lent half the sum for a down payment. The remaining two hundred fifty must be paid during the year, together with the personal loan from the Hampton treasurer.

To Booker T. Washington the sum seemed

Tuskegee Institute, founded in 1881 by Booker T. Washington, was the home of George Washington Carver for 50 years.

enormous. In these days of easier money it is impossible to realize how hard it was then for a black to raise any money at all. Miss Davidson, one of the early teachers, took in some by holding suppers at Tuskegee. She canvassed the town families, white and black, and everyone gave food, a cake, a pie, rice, a chicken. She and the others raked in by pennies the sum required.

Those first years were hard. The campus was a forest, and had to be cleared before it could be used for a school. There was no money to hire woodcutters, and the teachers Mr. Washington engaged were unwilling to chop wood.

Booker T. Washington solved the problem by setting out with an axe over his shoulder. His teachers could not refuse to follow their head. They cleared twenty acres and planted a crop. They also made bricks and put up buildings. Thus building and brickmaking became Institute courses. In the same way other departments rose out of school needs.

Since the school had no money to buy the wagon it needed, a wheelwright's course was started. Since the school bill for tinware was too large, an ex-slave, who had been one of the first men to dream of this school, brought his tin-smith business to the campus and taught the craft. This Lewis Adams taught harnessmaking and shoemaking as well, having been well trained in slavery days.

At first the students slept on ticking sacks stuffed with pine needles, but soon a mattress-making course was installed and produced good beds for the dormitory while teaching the students the trade. Dr. Washington's brother, seeing bees fly over the campus, got them to swarm in a packing box, and began a course in bee culture which supplied the dining hall with honey for years.

While the students had been required to grow most of their food, the farming courses were unpopular. These boys had not fought their way to school in order to keep on with the same work they had been doing. They were not the only ones who belittled agriculture. It was only beginning to be considered a science. Farmers had lately begun to inoculate pigs for cholera and cows for tuberculosis. They had just begun to use ensilage, preserving green fodder in its own juices, as the housewife preserves sauerkraut. Very new was the serious study of giving strength back to the soil by changing from one crop to another and by using fertilizers. And the nation was being startled by the new idea as to the critical importance of topsoil. "Uncle Henry" Wallace had made a strong statement about it, when he said that countries lasted only as long as their topsoil.

Booker T. Washington was convinced that agriculture was one of the most important studies Tuskegee could teach. At first he took it for granted that a white director would be needed; that no black had the training. When he learned about Professor Carver, he offered him the position, at a salary of fifteen hundred dollars a year.

George Carver realized all too well what it would mean to him to accept the offer. Most of the people around Tuskegee were poor and uneducated, and an educated black was treated the same as the uneducated. In Tuskegee he would lose the gracious contacts he so prized at Ames, the general respect and friendship.

He did not dare think of the contrast. He must think only that his dream school had come to life and was calling him. Sorrowfully, he accepted the offer.

Ames bade the young man farewell with deep regret and Tuskegee received him with indifference. A group of students were sitting on the steps of the first men's dormitory, barnlike old Porter Hall, when a one-horse dray drove up from the railway station at Chehaw, five miles away. In the dray, astride a tin-covered trunk, sat a striking young man. He was tall and thin. His gray suit was skimpy, so that his long hands dangled below his cuffs and his well-blacked work shoes were just as noticeable below his trousers. His nose was a proud high beak, but the mouth half hidden by a well-kept mustache was gentle and the eyes which ruled the whole face were smiling ones. The pink rose in his lapel completed his unusual appearance.

The students were even more astonished at him when he spoke, his voice was so unusually high and soft. "Young men," he asked, "where may I find Mr. Washington's office?"

One of the boys asked what class the newcomer was expecting to enter at Tuskegee.

"Young man," Mr. Carver answered, "Mr.
Washington has asked me to come here as one of
his instructors."

Still more amazed, the boys pointed out the
office. As Mr. Carver went on, one of them muttered, "Well, this is one time I think B.T. has
made a mistake."

That first day Tuskegee impressed Mr. Carver
as little as Mr. Carver impressed Tuskegee. After
tidy, fertile Ames, this campus shocked him. It
was crisscrossed by great gullies, torn in the red,
yellow, gray and purple Alabama soil. The country round Tuskegee seemed blighted, with its un-
painted, shackly cabins and general air of poverty.
The people looked crude, untidy, sick. They were
sick. Many of them were weak with pellagra, a
disease caused by their poor diet of corn meal and
pork.

At once Professor Carver saw one reason for
the poverty and sickness. This district, like the
rest of the South, was drained by the one-crop
system. For years cotton had sucked the earth dry
of food, and yearly the fields were burned over to
prepare them for the next planting. Thus they lost
even the little food they might have got if the old
stalks had been ploughed under. Besides, the cot-

ton was planted up to the very doors of the tenant farmers. They had no place for even the small gardens that would have given them fresh green vegetables.

First this misery and waste saddened Professor Carver, and next it excited him like a challenge. And as he talked over the conditions with his new chief, he was strengthened by the feeling that they were two men with one goal: the uplift of their race.

Booker T. Washington was only a few years older than his new department head. He was a fiery, strong-faced young man, who set his heart on doing big things quickly and demanded the same zeal and hard work from everyone on his staff. To him and to Tuskegee George Carver pledged himself. He made only one condition: when he had developed the department so that it could be handed over to someone else, he would return to his painting. After all his attempts to give it up, art still held him. He felt, too, that by painting in addition to doing scientific work he could show the world what blacks could accomplish "in science, literature and art."

The first thing needed for his teaching science was a laboratory. The building was there, but it was empty, and there was no money to buy the usual costly apparatus.

Professor Carver demanded the same zeal and hard work from his students that he demanded from himself.

"We'll make what we need," the new professor told his thirteen pupils.

"What out of?" they asked blankly.

"Out of things we'll find," their teacher replied.

He led them on a scavenger hunt to school and town dumps. They knocked at back doors, asking for leaky kettles, discarded jars, old rubber. Some pupils snickered and some sulked, but they all went, since Professor Carver led the way.

As soon as they had gathered a good assortment of junk, he set to work with it. He showed his class how jars and bottles could be cut down into retorts and beakers, and how useful a cracked cup could be as a mortar. He made an alcohol lamp out of an ink bottle, and pipettes from reeds which he gathered in the swamp. An old tin shingle with different-sized holes punched in it became a grader. The wild bamboo was made to order for their needs. He cut a square opening between each two joints, slipped in a piece of glass for a window, and had a display case for various types of soil.

Even while outfitting his laboratory, he was working on the soil problem, to help the wretched neighborhood farmers. In this purpose his chief agreed with him, but he urged him not to neglect the campus wells, the cattle, which gave little milk, the poultry, the proposed orchard, the repair of the school wagons.

Professor Carver felt that his greatest duty was to the farmers, and he put it first, often to Mr. Washington's impatience.

Professor Carver brought in samples of soil from the neighborhood farms and analyzed them to find what could be added to better them, and what crops they would best grow. He found all the soils poor, ranging from coarse sand to sandy or clayey loam.

He planned to have bulletins printed in the school shop and given to the farmers. These bulletins would explain how anyone could improve the harmful pork and corn meal diet by cooking the greens that grew free along every roadside. The bulletins would tell how to prepare the greens so that they would be tasty as well as prevent pellagra. They would also tell in simple words about the soil's need for food, and how to feed it.

There was an obstacle. Few of the farmers could read. For those who could not, Professor Carver "wrote" a different kind of bulletin, twenty acres across. He and his class tilled a field and showed what could be done with soil so poor that the school strawberry patch yielded only a cupful of berries a day.

He had found one place on the campus where vegetation throve. On the dump where he had gathered laboratory equipment pumpkin vines grew and bore fine pumpkins. Thinking of these, Professor Carver concluded that not alone animal manure and vegetable waste but any kind of decaying matter was food for hungry soil.

He set his students to making compost heaps. Grumbling, they piled up all sorts of rubbish, covered it with leaves, and left it to decay. That was for the future, for tomorrow.

For today, Mr. Carver requested a two-horse plow. Everyone laughed at the demand, for plowing was still done the old way in Macon County with a simple plow drawn by a single ox or horse. However, the professor got his plow and broke the ground thoroughly. Then he had his class bring swamp muck and barnyard manure and spread them over the red, yellow and purple earth. Finally, he had them plant the acre in cowpeas.

They laughed again at the small crop he harvested after all his trouble. Professor Carver cheerfully cooked the despised cowpeas and served them to his boys, who were astonished to find them good.

Next the professor planted sweet potatoes on the same ground, and, after the sweet potatoes, cotton of a strain he had been working on. The first year the Institute farm lost $16.25. The second year it earned $4.00, the third, $75 an acre from two crops of sweet potatoes. When from an acre of the worthless ground Professor Carver harvested the unheard-of crop of a five-hundred-pound bale of cotton, people stopped laughing. Maybe there was something in the man's wild ideas, after all.

By this time Professor Carver needed equipment which he could not find on the dump. He decided to use what he had, in another sense of the word, and make out of it what he wanted. He had music! In striped trousers and frock coat he made a concert tour of the South, "Professor Carver at the piano."

From this journey and from his growing acquaintance with the region round Tuskegee, Professor Carver gained new vision into the needs of southern farmers. Mr. Washington, born and reared in the South, had early understood those needs and set himself to fill them. Yearly, he had held a Farmer's Conference at Tuskegee, its aim to lead his people to make not only good farms but also good homes, good schools, good churches and good lives.

Yet the Conference, Professor Carver saw, did not go far enough. That was the trouble; it did not "go," and many of the farmers could not or would not come.

So, when Professor Carver had been ten years at Tuskegee, the first Movable School of Agriculture, which he designed, began to go to the farmers. One of his best pupils, Thomas Monroe Campbell, was in charge. That first wagon carried cream separator, churn, plows and garden tools. Later a cow was added and a crate with a common razorback hog in one end and a purebred sow in the other. The people gathered at school,

In 1906, in his early 40s and after ten years at Tuskegee, Carver launched the first Movable School of Agriculture—a traveling classroom for poor, rural farmers.

church or farmhouse and spent the day learning new skills, not only farming and care of farm tools, but whitewashing houses, caring for sick-rooms, building henhouses.

The work of the Booker T. Washington School

on Wheels, as it was sometimes called, proved so effective that the United States Department of Agriculture employed Mr. Campbell to direct similar work in seven southern states.

In 1918 an automobile truck was put into use in the project. It was named the Knapp Truck, after Seaman Knapp, grandfather of the little boy who had brought his friends to the Ames greenhouse to meet George Carver. The descendants of that first horse-drawn, secondhand buggy of Professor Carver's, with its homemade exhibit stands, were to be powerful motor trucks which would make the Knapp Truck look small and the buggy laughable. And they were to go far afield, not only throughout America, but to distant Africa.

7

Out of What You Have

ALL THIS TIME Professor Carver was fitting into his new setting. Some of it he could fit to himself instead. In his second year he landscaped the campus. He had it graded and terraced, and planted Bermuda grass to cloak it with green. He set trees and shrubs and swift-growing honeysuckle and wistaria to cover the steep banks.

Other things about Tuskegee were as unlike Ames as the campus was. As he searched fields, woods and roadsides for plants, the townspeople often spoke kindly to him. They called him "Uncle," their title for all respectable blacks past boyhood. Sometimes they asked him to cut their lawns or spade their gardens. Occasionally he did so, because it was easier than explaining who he was and why he wandered around with his arms full of weeds.

The neighboring blacks soon came to know him. Puzzlingly different from anyone they had met before, they found him able to help them when they tramped to the Institute to tell him their troubles. Soon they, too, were calling him "Doctor," though with another meaning from his Diamond Grove neighbors and his Ames classmates. These Alabama farmers thought him a "root doctor" like their own, who treated with charms and potions as well as herbs and roots.

Even when he cured them, some still puzzled about him. Others had no feelings except gratitude and admiration, and welcomed him eagerly when he came to sit awhile in their cabins, noticing their needs and suggesting helpful changes.

His healing fame brought him all kinds of patients. Two little boys lugged their hurt dog to "Doctah," their bare feet white with dust, their faces streaked with sweat, tears and the dirt of the long road. The dog was a cur, but their pet and friend, and Doctah gently promised to do what he could for it if they would leave it with him. When they came back, it was on the way to recovery. He cured Booker T. Washington's favorite riding horse, and often traced down some baffling illness in hogs and chickens. Anything alive was of interest to him, and anything that mattered to another human being mattered to Dr. Carver.

Dr. Carver. First Carvers' George, with no surname of his own. Then George Carver, when he went out into the world and needed a name to go by. Then Mr. Carver, as he earned the respect of friends and acquaintances. Next Professor Carver, because the title belonged to him. Finally Dr. Carver, because that handle seemed to fit his name, though not formally his.

Though the Institute found the new teacher hard to understand, they soon learned to like him. He became popular even with those who did not guess his worth. Here, as at Ames, his dining table was the gayest in the room. It was his idea to celebrate the birthdays of everyone at the table, and for each he painted cards and planned something special. When three of them had birthdays the same month he protested, ''We want a party every month. After this we'll ask everyone his birth-date before we let him join us.''

He loved to joke. He enjoyed tussling with ''his boys,'' and would give them a good paddling when the fun ran high. This was the first time he had been in a community made up of his own people, and while he missed his wide circle of friends in the North, this easy sociability had charm.

His associates waited hopefully for him to find romance at Tuskegee. In upper classes and staff there were eligible girls, some of them beautiful, bright and gifted. Dr. Carver seemed to have little time for them, except to teach them. Though there are rumors of an unsuccessful courtship, it seems more probable that Dr. Carver early put aside all thought of love and marriage. He loved humanity, and he was married to a lifelong task. He believed he was not meant to have home and family.

Yet home life was dear to him. For years he had Thanksgiving dinner regularly with the family of a fellow professor. Dr. Carver was quietly happy when a child of this family was named after him, and he mourned the stillness in the house when one after another the children went out into the world.

After a few years Dr. Washington offered him an increase in his fifteen-hundred-dollar salary. Dr. Carver refused it. What use had he for money? He had all God's universe to draw on for his needs. He believed that God had made a world that would supply his children's every want, if only they would take the trouble to use it.

Once he was asked, "Dr. Carver, what are you? Would you call yourself a scientist? An agriculturalist? A chemist?"

Dr. Carver answered, "I am a master of things."

He was not bragging. He was taking literally

the words in the Eighth Psalm, in the Bible he read so much:

> Thou hast made him—man—but little lower than
>   God,
> And crownest him with glory and honor.
>
> Thou makest him to have dominion over the works
>   of Thy hands.

Humble before the Great Maker, he was never humble before things. He was Master of Things, and therefore felt small need of money, that man-made medium of exchange.

His indifference bothered the Institute treasurer. Dr. Carver upset the bookkeeping by failing to cash his salary checks. Once when asked to give to a worthy cause, Dr. Carver explained that he had no money. Then a thought struck him and he rummaged in his crowded desk. "This might help," he added, "and this, and this." He handed the astonished caller forgotten salary checks amounting to several hundred dollars.

There really were few things for which he needed money. After college days, clothes did not interest him and he spent little for them. He did buy shoes and other needed garments for boys and girls who came to Tuskegee poorly dressed and with empty pockets. Some he helped with

Throughout his career at Tuskegee, Dr. Carver experimented with soil enrichment and the cultivation of crops that might prove profitable for Southern farmers.

their tuition. On little George Carver Campbell's birthdays, for fifteen years or so, Dr. Carver enjoyed putting a five-dollar bill into the boy's hand, "for the educational fund." It was at George's home that Dr. Carver always spent Thanksgiving.

Except for such uses, money did not interest him. When Dr. Washington—who often borrowed from him if short of cash—insisted on his cashing his salary checks, the money piled up in his bank account, untouched. His disappointment may have been mixed with amusement when years later the bank failed and he lost a tidy little fortune. "See what happens to money when you hoard it?"

During his first ten years at Tuskegee he busily experimented with soil improvement, with sweet potatoes, cowpeas, velvet beans and cotton, and with grains which might be profitable to the South. He also had courses to teach, and practical matters to attend to, outside of the research in which he was so brilliant.

Dr. Carver was finding Dr. Washington hard to work with, much as he admired him. These great men were opposites, except in love of learning and devotion to their people. Dr. Washington was the hard-hitting man of affairs, impatient of delays, Dr. Carver the scholar, thinking and working with insight and infinite pains. After fifteen years together the two reached the breaking point. It was well for Dr. Carver and for the world that they did. Dr. Washington did not want to lose Dr. Carver and Dr. Carver still felt bound to Tuskegee. Yet both could see that Dr. Carver could not go on in his present position, where the variety of tasks required of him kept him from devoting the needed time and attention to the research which he knew to be his most important work. A new department was made, to solve the difficulty. It was the Department of Agricultural Research, with Dr. Carver in complete charge. After that he was freer to develop his great talents for the good of humanity.

The new position was supposed to relieve him of all teaching, but students begged for classes with him and would not be refused. For many more years he continued to teach a limited number. Loving young people and seeing their possibilities, he was able to inspire as well as instruct them.

After he became Director of Research the news of his discoveries spread abroad more generally. He was asked to address churches, clubs and other organizations far and wide, and to take his exhibits to fairs and conventions.

It was his experiments with peanuts that brought him his first wide fame.

He had always tried to improve conditions on southern farms. He disliked the one-crop system, with nothing but cotton planted. King Cotton destroyed soil, plantation owners and tenant farmers by taking all the nutriment from the ground where it grew. Yet Dr. Carver felt that the time for his overthrow had not yet come. Farmers could not be made to believe that other crops would serve them better.

Therefore he compromised, perfecting more profitable kinds of cotton by crossing valuable long-staple cotton with the sturdier short-staple. One bush would bear two hundred and seventy-five huge bolls, without use of commercial fertilizer.

Agriculturalists began to seek him out. The Colonial Secretary of the German Empire spent days at Tuskegee consulting him, and an Australian took the remarkable new seed to his government, which introduced it in Australia. Distant farmers sent him specimens of their soil and well water for analysis. He always answered with thoughtful advice. A group of pecan growers, their groves dying of an unknown disease, sought Dr. Carver's help. His suggested treatment saved them from ruin,—but Dr. Carver politely returned the check they sent him.

At last the day he had expected came, when King Cotton's throne tottered. For years the boll weevil had been marching northward from Mexico like an army, boring into the cotton bolls and destroying the cotton before it could ripen. No one could prevent the destruction, but Dr. Carver believed he could rebuild after they had torn down, at the same time helping to end the one-crop system. There were crops that would grow well in Alabama's poor soil and at the same time feed it instead of draining it as cotton did. Among these were the velvet bean, good for stock feed, and the soy bean, with its hundred uses, almost unnoticed then, except by Dr. Carver.

Dr. Carver knew people as well as plants. He knew it would take many years to coax them to plant unfamiliar crops. So he proposed a plant as familiar as an old shoe, the peanut. Every garden had a peanut patch, for everyone liked peanuts, though nobody thought them important.

The plant has unusual ways. When the flower withers, the stem lengthens and bends, pushing the seed pod into the ground to ripen. Like other members of the pea family, it has queer roots. These roots bear small swellings or tubercles, containing bacteria-like matter which has the ability to take nitrogen from the air and hold it in a form the plants can use. For this reason such plants are good to grow in orchards or between the rows of fields in poor soil. Either by the decay of their roots or by the plowing under of the plants, they enrich the earth.

When the boll weevil arrived, Dr. Carver stood ready to defend Macon County, Alabama. His weapon was a peanut.

He told the farmers to plow up their infected cotton and destroy it. They must spray the ground where it had grown, let it stand idle for a month, and plant peanuts on it. After fifteen years, the farmers had learned to respect Dr. Carver's judgment, and many of them did as he said. The first result was deep trouble for Dr. Carver.

The peanut harvest was the largest in the history of Alabama, and there was no market for it. Peanuts were sold at the circus, with popcorn and pink lemonade, and a few were made into the novelty spread, peanut butter. But the demand was small, and supplied by imports from the Orient.

The problem was first brought to Professor Carver by a widow who had followed his suggestion and now had a large crop, useless on her hands. Dr. Carver was deeply concerned, feeling that he had given advice without looking far enough ahead.

However, it was his habit to make use of his misfortunes. So, since he always depended on God to give him what he needed, he went to his laboratory, which he called God's Little Workshop, and had a talk with his Creator. Humbly he asked what the peanut was and what it was meant for.

He was never long in doubt of God's answers to his questions. This time he felt that God was telling him to take the peanut apart and find out just what it held for him to work with. That would be easy, after his years of practice in resolving things into their elements.

First he went out after a supply of peanuts. Then he drew guards over his sweater sleeves, put on his flour-sack apron, and went to work.

He shelled a double handful of peanuts, laying the hulls aside for further experiment, and ground the nuts fine. Then he heated part of them and put them in a cotton bag and under a press, which he screwed down till it had extracted all the oil it could.

The cake that remained looked dry, but Dr. Carver knew that it retained some oil. Long fingers flying, he added a solvent which released the last bit of the oil. It was wonderful stuff, as he had long known. Most of the animal fats had a gelatinous membrane around each oil particle, but this had none. It was therefore much easier to break down its fat globules.

He worked with such interest and concentration that he only dimly heard repeated soft tappings at the door, and footsteps hesitantly retreating into the distance. Now a more decisive knock broke through his veil of absorption. It was followed by a voice which coaxed and scolded at the same time.

"Doctor, didn't you know that dinner time was long past? Better you come and eat."

"Hmmm?" he murmured gently, still peering down the beak of his nose at his peanuts.

"Doctor! We been keeping your dinner warm, but it's going to dry up for sure."

"Don't worry. I'm not at all hungry," he murmured again, hardly noticing his own words.

Once more the steps retreated, only to return. "Doctor," the voice pleaded, "please let me in. I've fetched you a tray."

"Well, I declare. I declare. Set it down, please. And thank you. Thank you."

The tray thumped to the floor, and Doctor sighed with relief, as if a nagging mosquito had left him at peace.

From some of the ground peanuts he had extracted a fluid that looked like creamy Jersey milk. It not only looked like milk, but analysis showed it to be milk, even though no cow, goat, or other animal grew on its family tree. What was more, a small glassful of shelled peanuts produced a pint. And if he was not mistaken it had every value that cow's milk had, except for calcium, which it possessed in smaller proportion. All the lines of Doctor's face curved upward in grateful satisfaction as he set it to one side.

The dry cake he put into another vessel, together with water and an enzyme, one of those mysterious digestive substances the animal bodies manufacture. This he set at a heat which would hold it at body temperature, so that the proteins should be separated from other elements.

He had absent-mindedly turned on the lights and continued with his work, dimly aware from time to time that voices grumbled and coaxed outside his locked door. When the doorknob rattled sharply he only muttered under his breath.

The artificial process of digestion was reasonably rapid. In a few hours he could tell that the peanut was rich in protein. It would take a much longer series of experiments to sort out the different kinds of amino acids that made up the protein. He must be sure that there were at least sixteen, so that it would fill all nutritional requirements.

Suddenly he was so tired that he paused in his work. His windowpanes were completely black, and all noises had seeped away, leaving a great silence. He glanced at his watch and murmured, "Well, I declare!" Strange how the hours had raced past.

Stealthily he unlocked his door and opened it a crack. All was dark and still outside, and the trays reproached him from the floor. He lifted them and carried them into his room, locked the door again and sat down to eat what he could of his cold dinner and supper. For a few minutes he sat relaxed, bowed shoulders sagging, head sunk on breast. Then, rested and refreshed, he piled the dishes neatly on the trays, set them outside, locked the door, and went back eagerly to his work.

The gray light of morning had drained the brightness from his electric bulbs when he inspected the beaker where he had poured his peanut milk the evening before. He chuckled. A rich coating of cream covered it. He skimmed off the cream and noted with pleasure that the milk showed no separation or curdling. Deftly he whipped the cream and chuckled anew. Sweet and fresh though it was, it formed a tiny lump of good butter. When he had time he would see what kind of cheese this vegetable milk would make. Now he must proceed with the isolating and identifying of the other elements of the peanut.

All that day he worked, sometimes making no reply at all to the urgent voices at the door. When he found himself too nearly exhausted to work longer without food, he would cautiously take in another tray, eat a little from it and return renewed. For two days and two nights he went on asking what the peanut was and what it was for. At last he emerged, gray and shaking with weariness but serenely joyful.

He had sorted out the contents of the tight little package that was the peanut. He had found water, fats, oils, gums, resins, sugars, starches, pectins, pentosans and proteins. He had recombined these elements at different heats and under different pressures, and had worked out twenty usable products from them. The biggest possible peanut harvest could be used with profit.

Even then he did not stop asking. He went on rearranging the substances—making what he wanted out of what he had—until he had discovered over three hundred useful peanut products.

He had long experimented with cookery on a stove in his laboratory. He made recipes for every kind of wild green and many for wild plums, to save the fruit otherwise wasted in years of large crops. Somewhat as he had planned when a child, he had classes in Home Economics, and among other things he taught ways to prepare peanuts for the table. As a climax, he had his girls serve Dr. Washington and other guests a five course peanut luncheon. The menu was soup, mock chicken, peanuts creamed as a vegetable, bread, ice cream, cookies, coffee and candy. The only item that did not contain peanuts was the salad, of pepper grass, sheep sorrel and chicory.

Among the three hundred products were the "rich Jersey milk" drinks, including instant coffee, Worcestershire and other sauces, flour, mixed pickles, salve, bleach, face cream, shaving cream, wallboard, synthetic rubber, linoleum. He sent samples of the face cream to several ladies, and while most of them were delighted, one protested that it was fattening her face.

The criticism gave Dr. Carver a new idea. If peanut oil fed the tissues of the face, would it not also feed wasted muscles? Long before, when he served as masseur for Iowa State athletes, he found no oils that suited him. Now he rejoiced in making several grades, from light to heavy. They were soon selling well, though, as usual, Dr. Carver refused to accept any profit from them.

He did have the joy of trying them himself on children and adults paralyzed by polio, and finding by measurement that their wasted limbs gained faster under massage with his peanut oil than with other oils. Some who had been badly crippled walked again without help after the peanut-oil treatment. The Institute Hospital had a polio unit, and even in his frail old age Dr. Carver went there each week and gave valuable time and strength to massaging serious cases.

The use of peanut oil for polio brought him sorrow as well as joy. Many newspapers published it as the hoped-for cure, bringing a flood of letters to Dr. Carver. Parents who had seen their children's bodies wrecked by the disease wrote to him for his "cure." In vain he published the facts: that his oil was on trial; that he made no great claims for it; that the massage and the patient's courage and faith were as important as the oil. In spite of all he could say, he received four thousand letters, begging for information, for help, for oil. Later it appeared more and more probable that Dr. Carver's own manipulation was the most vital factor in the improvement of his young patients, though the oil itself was admittedly superior.

Meanwhile, the peanut milk proved an unquestionable blessing. The great Indian leader, Gandhi, found it a healthful food, as well as the soybean formula Dr. Carver worked out for him. In Africa the milk saved lives. If an African mother died when her child was born, the child also died. Or if the mother lived but could not nurse her baby, there was no way to raise it. That was because wild animals and tsetse flies prevent the keeping of cows. Now the missionaries fed starving babies on Dr. Carver's peanut milk, and they grew plump and strong.

Carver developed nearly 300 products—all of them useful, many of them important—from the ordinary peanut.

It proved well suited to cheesemaking, also. While it takes a hundred pounds of cow's milk to make ten pounds of cheese, only thirty-three pounds of peanut milk are required.

By 1921 the peanut industry had become so important that the tariff on peanuts also became important. Almost half the supply was shipped from China and Japan, and the duty was only three-eighths of a cent a pound on the unshelled, and three-fourths of a cent on the shelled. American growers felt that four and five cents duty was needed to cover the difference in cost between coolie and American labor. So the Peanut Grower's Association asked Carver to show the possibilities of the peanut to the Ways and Means Committee of the House of Representatives.

George Washington Carver went to Washington.

He had a wooden box in which he carried twenty-five or thirty specimens of his peanut exhibit. This case he always packed and lugged himself. Arriving in the Washington railway station, he found no one to meet him, and asked a redcap to help him to a cab with his box. The redcap was friendly but busy. "Sorry, grandpop," he said, "but I'm supposed to pick up some great scientist from Alabama and take him to the Capitol."

Dr. Carver doubtless chuckled inwardly, but he was too stubborn to explain the mistake. Finally he found a taxi that could take him and his box, and they started out. He had time for sightseeing on the way, and the driver, though amused, was good-natured. At his fare's request, he drove through the botanical gardens, and stopped when asked. Dr. Carver had caught sight of a rare shrub infected with a dangerous disease. Before he could be stopped, he was breaking off sick branches, clucking to himself. When an official had been called, Dr. Carver pointed out the evidence of disease, told the official that it must have come into this country in plants from Far Eastern jungles, and explained how to wipe it out. The Washington botanist gave grateful attention.

When Dr. Carver reached the House of Representatives, he sat quietly in the rear and listened to endless fussing and reading of briefs. He was uneasy over having to talk to so disorderly a crowd. Besides, it was almost four o'clock, and four o'clock was closing time.

At last peanuts came on the docket, and the Virginia-Carolina Co-operative Peanut Exchange attested that a "protective tariff on peanuts was the only thing that could save the sandy-land farmers from ruin." George W. Carver's name was called and he lugged his heavy case to the platform. Representatives sprawled yawning in their seats and then straightened to gape at the elderly black man slowly mounting the steps.

"Your time has been cut to ten minutes," the chairman said.

He had come all this way for ten minutes. Many speakers would have protested indignantly. Dr. Carver had always said, "Make what you want out of what you have." Now he had ten minutes, an audience of bored men, his array of peanut products and his self-control, wit, gentle fun-making. With these he went to work.

His clear, silvery voice pierced the stale air like a bird song and sleepy lawmakers stopped their yawns in the middle. "I've been asked to tell about the extension of the peanut," Dr. Carver began, "but we'll have to hurry if we are to extend it, because in ten minutes you will tell me to stop."

With practiced speed he unpacked his products. He held up a chocolate candy and popped it into his mouth with a joke about having to enjoy it for them. They stopped yawning. This was a good show after hours of dull debate.

First he told them that the peanut and the sweet potato were twin brothers. If all other foods were taken away, these twins would give man everything needed for healthful diet. He showed a sirup made from sweet potato and used with peanuts to make a candy bar. He showed them stock feed, ice cream ready to freeze, linoleum. When he had them fascinated, he remarked meekly that his ten minutes were up. They insisted on his having more time.

So, keeping them amused with jokes, he went on. He showed peanut milk, covered with thick cream, and cereal coffee, whose flavor he had

enriched by repeated roastings. He showed but-
termilk, and evaporated milk such as had saved
the African babies. He showed face cream, meat
substitutes, wood dyes. His ten minutes
stretched to an hour and three-quarters, and his
whole audience was wide awake and asking interested questions.

When one Representative scoffingly asked
what Dr. Carver knew about tariffs, Dr. Carver
jokingly retorted, "This is all the tariff means: to
shut the other fellow out."

That was all he said about it, but after seeing
his exhibition the committee wrote into the pend-
ing bill the best tariff rate the American peanut
growers had ever had.

Besides his other discoveries, Dr. Carver had
found how to make peanut butter that could be
kept much longer than the earlier product. This
improvement, along with a better understanding
of its food value, turned it from a picnic novelty
into a staple item of diet.

As a result of all this development, the peanut
crop gradually worked up to a value second only
to that of cotton, and the one-crop system was
ended. An interesting example of the change is
Dothan, Alabama, the "capital of the peanut
belt." The peanut boosted the town's population
from a thousand or less to twenty-one thousand,

its main industry being the extraction of peanut oil for butter, salad dressing and other products.

Maxwell County actually put up a monument to the boll weevil, because that pest had forced them to stop raising cotton and start raising peanuts. To use the slang phrase, the peanut business is no longer ''peanuts.'' All this has flowed indirectly from Dr. Carver's Little Workshop. Small wonder he was called the Peanut Wizard.

8

I Am Master of Things

THE PEANUT WIZARD was far more than the name implied. He had gone on experimenting, working wonders along many lines.

The sweet potato, as he had told the House of Representatives, is a good partner to the peanut. It also grows well in sandy soil. In addition, it has many elements which can be "shuffled" in different heats and pressures, to form new substances.

From it Dr. Carver developed over a hundred useful products, fewer than from the peanut because it contains no oil. The sweet potato is made up of one part ash, or waste, sixty-nine parts water and thirty parts sugar, starch, cellulose and fat.

During World War I Dr. Carver produced an excellent sweet-potato flour for use at Tuskegee. The bread made from it was good and widely used, and saved so much wheat for shipping overseas that Dr. Carver was called to Washington to confer about it with Army chemists and bakers.

At that time America found herself left without good dyes. Germany had long supplied our dyestuffs, and when importations were cut off we were helpless. The first dyes made by our chemists were poor substitutes. Bright, gay ginghams colored with them faded to dingy drab after a few washings. Dr. Carver worked out fine, fast dyes from sweet potato, as well as from many other common substances: clays, dandelions, black oak, wood ashes, grapes, onions and tomato vines.

During the Second World War he found another good use for the sweet potato: to make fine starch for the manufacture of paste for stamps and envelope flaps. For this paste tapioca had been imported in large quantities. Small as a postage stamp is, the amount of paste used on the yearly output is huge. The sweet-potato substitute was of great value. Again Dr. Carver was asked to speak before Congress, and this time his subject was the sweet potato.

He often sent samples of his work to Dr. Pammell, one of his beloved teachers at Iowa State. Once he sent three samples made from rotten sweet potatoes, velvet beans and china-berries. Differently used, he wrote, they became wood stains, water-color paints, dye for wool, and a substance for ebonizing wood. Here were materials that were always overabundant. Sweet potatoes grew well and kept poorly. Velvet beans, raised for fertilizer and for feed, were easily grown. The china-berry trees spread their green parasols everywhere in the South, clouds of pink-lavender fragrance in summer, followed by showers of ill-smelling berries in fall.

Things that were usually wasted were a challenge to Dr. Carver. From wood shavings he made synthetic marble so good that promotors formed a marble company and begged him to come to them as consultant. When he refused, they brought their company to Tuskegee in order to be near him and have his advice.

From pecan shells he made milk, condiments, axle grease and seventy different dyes for silk and cotton. From the sludge left after benzine, gasoline and naphtha had been taken from crude oil, he made both rubber and dye. He found that the waste from most farm produce could be made into paper. Most of the paper on which he painted his pictures he made from corn or okra stalks. Since almost all vegetable growth contains cellulose, out of which paper is made, Dr. Carver thought it cruel waste to cut down forests of slow-growing timber for the paper mills.

When the Second World War came on, Dr.

Carver turned his attention to synthetic rubber. In a world that ran on rubber tires, a rubber shortage could be deadly.

The greater use of cotton also absorbed Dr. Carver in his later years. The market was choked with cotton and needed more outlets for it. Woven cotton was tried as a binder in road-building and proved practical, but Dr. Carver worked out a way to make a stronger, cheaper paving block using raw cotton with only the valuable seed removed. Thus forty bales could be used to the mile, instead of only six or eight, as when it was made into cloth.

It has often been claimed that no man has ever given the world so much wealth as Dr. Carver. Here was one man, alone. With no group of scientists to work out his ideas, no rich organization behind him. He dreamed of things that had never been done. Entirely alone, he shuffled the elements of simple substances and found countless new products, many of them immensely valuable.

The sale of patents and the royalties from his discoveries would have made him enormously wealthy if he had been willing to take out patents. But since the knowledge had been given to him, he gave it freely to the world.

He gave mankind health as well as wealth. He

never tired of showing his neighbors how cheaply they could have wholesome food that would keep them well. In a few years pellagra, a serious deficiency disease, was almost gone from Macon County. His bulletins had described the use of a hundred common grasses and weeds for appetizing food. His experiments in canning and drying had showed how to keep the summer surplus for the lean winter days. His peanut milk and oils added their bit to heal human bodies and save lives.

Dr. Carver's heart had been weakened by early illnesses and constant overwork. Not only at Tuskegee but all over the world his friends grew anxious about him. Henry Ford had an elevator put in at the door of his little apartment, so that he need not climb the stairs. His "exquisite elevator," Dr. Carver chucklingly called it, enjoying it as if it had been a new plaything.

No, health was never his, yet he gave it to the world in great, generous handfuls.

Another of his gifts, most notable throughout his last twenty years, was the spirit of good will. More and more often he was asked to speak to all kinds of groups, in the South, where he was warmly welcomed, in the Midwest, and along the eastern coast. Illustrating with exhibits, he lectured on such topics as "The Earth Is Full of

Riches.'' He won his hearers, even when at first they were hostile. The young were as responsive as their elders, for his power to waken youth to its own possibilities was always remarkable. One summer when he was on the staff of a Youth Conference, his whole group formed the habit of getting up before five, in order to share his early morning walks. Increasing numbers of boys followed him, for he made their world shine with fresh beauty and wonder. Everything he saw, heard, smelled, was of use and interest.

''He would pick up a common weed that I hadn't even noticed,'' recalls Jack Boyd, a leader in that conference. ''He'd pull it apart, saying, 'Now if you ever give yourself a cut when you're shaving, just put on some of this juice. It's antiseptic.' ''

In many cases the inspiration of his personality was lasting. Boys who had heard him came to Tuskegee for two days or two weeks, in order to hear more. Many applied to study under him. If they were white it was impossible, since Alabama law made it illegal for whites and blacks to study together. But they could write to him, and did, and he answered, busy though he was. From one Youth Conference seven boys wrote him nine hundred and four letters.

In addition to his teaching and administrative duties, laboratory work, land improvement, and crop cultivation, Carver found time to grow flowers and other plants.

All across America, young people gave deep attention when he spoke, sometimes rising in a body to applaud him, as if he were a prophet. His words were not always gentle. In the fine city of Tulsa, Oklahoma, he had seen the young folks jazzing round with no apparent thought for anything but pleasure. "How much can the world depend on you?" he asked them sternly from the platform.

It may have been during that same visit that his early morning walks took him up Standpipe Hill. There he found twenty-seven varieties of medicinal plants, all of kinds that were being shipped in from outside sources by Tulsa druggists. They might as well be gathered for local use, he told the people, or for shipping out to other drugstores, thus creating a new industry.

After one of his stirring speeches, a Southerner made this comment: "I was taught by my father that a Negro child and a white child were the same up to their twelfth year; after that the white child began to advance, while the Negro child began to imitate. I want to ask my white friends tonight, Whom has this Negro imitated?"

Many of his listeners would have agreed with Ambrose Caliver, of the United States Office of Education. Mr. Caliver said that Dr. Carver "clarified my conception of God, deepened my spiritual life, strengthened my faith in humanity.'' He was, in truth, a messenger of good will.

Beauty was another gift which Dr. Carver believed the Maker had meant everyone to have free. Odds and ends of his time he spent in making odds and ends of things into furnishings that would lend grace to the poor cabins of the neighborhood. From okra, cornstalks, waste twine, he made rugs. No twine was waste twine to him, however. Every bit of it that came his way he rolled in neat balls. From the clays around him he made wood stains, so that the poorest farmer might have color in his cabin and upon it. He also showed his students and neighbors how to make a fine whitewash from the white clay abounding in the neighborhood. They were to sift it, so that it would be free of grit, and then put it into a gunnysack and draw it back and forth through a tub of water until the clay was held in suspension in the water. This simple procedure would give them a good wash for their buildings, if they had not time to make a more lasting paint.

However, he wanted paint, because it was more permanent than any wash. Even the cheapest paint cost too much for most of these farmers, especially since the soft resinous pine of their cabin walls drank paint greedily. Dr. Carver found the answer in waste automobile oil. He ground fine the bright regional clays, screened out the lumps, and mixed in crank-case oil. The result was durable paint that cost nothing but labor.

"Will these paints of yours hold their pretty colors?" people asked doubtfully.

Dr. Carver smiled at the question. "These colors have already lasted for thousands of years," he reminded them.

His eye for color was so keen that he could detect it in unlikely places. Near the campus lay a stretch of red earth. To others it was only red earth, but Dr. Carver saw, hidden in its carmine, a wonderful blue. He took some of the clay home to his laboratory. Again and again he oxidized it with heat, and each time got a "bluer" blue, until he had produced a pigment seventy times as blue as the ordinary color. Artists and scientists hailed it as the "Lost Blue," the Egyptian pigment which no one in modern times had been able to copy. In the old tombs they had found it, on decorated walls and ornaments, unfaded by centuries. Here it was again, a color at once soft, rich and intense.

Dr. Carver made all his own artists' paints out of the native clays, and he developed a new way of applying them. He put them on the canvas or paper with his thumbs rather than with brushes. The Luxembourg in Paris asked for one picture painted in that way. It is a study of peaches, so glowing, firm and juicy looking that one wants to bite into them.

His flowers continued to give another outlet for his love of beauty. The usual flower still bloomed in his buttonhole, and his windows were full of plants. In his later years he had a small conservatory behind his office. There he spent happy hours, crossing flowers to attain new colors and greater loveliness.

Up to the time when his doctors and his bodily weakness together forbade the lifelong practice, he went on rising at four and beginning the day's work in the thrilling hours of early morning. Usually he spent them in wood and field, seeking and finding new wonders.

Many of these wonders have never yet been used commercially. Some are experiments for the future. For example, as long as coffee is abundant and reasonably priced, it is not profitable to manufacture a substitute from pecan shells, but in times when the importation of the bean was cut off, such a substitute might be of great worth.

It is also noteworthy that there is usually a lag between a new discovery and its "catching on"— about twenty years before its manufacture and use begins. An example is the dehydration— water removal—of food, to save shipping space.

During World War I Dr. Carver proposed dehydration, to save the waste weight and space of the water content. He showed Army chemists his process, but not until World War II was the idea generally used.

Dr. Carver did not seem to care about getting the credit for his discoveries. He wanted to show what could be done. He said of himself, "I am only a trail-blazer." He was opening a broad path to a new era. This new era might be called the Synthetic Age. It might be called the Chemurgic Age.

The name chemurgy did not exist until 1935, when a great conference was held in Dearborn, Michigan, under the encouragement of Henry Ford. Chemists, physicists, economists, manufacturers, leaders in other fields, met to talk over ways of saving the dangerous waste of farm produce and labor.

It was not hard to see why the waste had increased. A hundred years ago four-fifths of everything used by men was grown on the farm. Then came the Machine Age, and demanded materials that could stand the great pressures of machinery. Since metals met that need, mining became more and more important. Today only one-third of what we use is grown on the farm.

While this change was taking place, chemists

were learning to increase vegetable growth enormously. In 1913 a German named Fritz Haber perfected a cheap way of taking nitrogen from the air, making the date 1913 perhaps more important than our 1776, or 1492. Agriculture had progressed greatly since 1840, when another German began to study the use of manure to restore strength to the soil; but fertilizer was expensive and its amount limited. With unlimited nitrogen, unlimited amounts of vegetation could be grown.

Plant life is not alone food for animals, including human beings: it is a trap for sunlight. It is nature's factory for turning sunlight, our only source of energy, into chemicals, out of which men can make anything and everything.

The Dearborn conference worked with this idea, that the farm could produce many things besides food. If it did, it would gain so large an outlet that it need never again fear overproduction. There would always be a market for all it could raise.

These scientists made it clear that our age is recklessly spending the stored wealth of millions of years, as if there were no end to the supply. Coal and oil are examples of the wealth under the earth's surface, as well as iron and other minerals. Millions of years were needed to compress vegetation into the carbon of coal; millions of years to gather the oil from organic matter. We have no way to deposit anything more in our great earth bank, yet we spend its funds without thought.

This spending of stored wealth has had a still more serious angle. One nation would think it must have the minerals, or oil, or rubber which another nation had cornered. So they fought for it, and spent vast sums of money and lives that could not be replaced.

The chemists at Dearborn believed chemistry could make from farm produce substitutes for the stored riches. In that way man could live on a pay-as-you-go basis, growing his own supplies from year to year. And since everyone could grow them, nations would not need to go to war for the possession of them.

Where does the name chemurgy come in? It denotes a new form of chemistry, and is a new name, coined from the Greek word *chemi*, chemistry, and the Greek word *ergon*, work. Chemurgy, pronounced KEM-er-ji, chemistry at work.

Of course the idea of making something out of something else is not new. Ancient Egypt used cooked starch plastics. Never before, however, had this definite attempt been made to grow all our goods on the farm.

Let us see how it has been working out. Oceans of milk have been wasted. A large propor-

tion of milk is casein, which forms the curd when
milk sours. Today there are made from this casein
coating for paper, paint, waterproof glue, pen
barrels, dishes, combs, buttons, artificial bone for
use in surgery, "ivory" jewelry, felt for hats,
"wool" for clothing.

Consider cotton. We have cotton-cement shin-
gles, cotton-asphalt road, cotton floors, wall tiles,
sheathing. So many uses are found for the oil that
bald-headed cotton is now grown for seeds alone.

Cellulose has been another object of chemurgic
study. Paper almost equals rubber and steel in
importance, for every man, woman and child of
us uses more than two hundred pounds of paper
yearly. We use and discard more than of anything
else except milk. First chemurgy found how to
make good paper from the southern pine, which
grows as large in twelve years as the Canadian
spruce, from which most paper has been made,
in fifty. Other uses are made of the cellulose
which is the base of paper. Made into liquid and
spun through tiny holes, it becomes rayon
thread. Forced through narrow slits, it becomes a
sheet of cellophane. Mixed with resin, it makes
car bodies with impact strength greater than that
of steel.

What has all this to do with Dr. Carver? Chemurgy is a road to which he pointed the way in

experiments back in 1890 and on. His three hundred peanut products and the hundred items made from sweet potatoes were forerunners of chemurgy.

Years earlier he had said, "I believe . . . that America is on the eve of the greatest scientific development it has ever known. . . . The ideal scientist of the future will be an investigator, one who dares to think independently, and unfolds before your eyes a veritable mystic maze of new and useful products."

The conference at Dearborn welcomed him to the speaker's platform as the "first and greatest chemurgist."

Plant Doctor, Peanut Wizard, Black Leonardo, First and Greatest Chemurgist:—Carvers' George.

9

With Glory and Honor

THE YEARS HAD MADE great changes since Professor Carver came to Tuskegee in 1896. They had made great changes in the world, in America, in Tuskegee, in George Washington Carver.

The campus of the Institute now delighted Dr. Carver. Its trees had grown to giant size: tall elms, mighty deodars, gum trees, magnolias. Shrubbery grew in pleasant groupings. Dogwood, redbud and china-berry in their season misted the green with color and fragrance. Even midwinter was sweet with camellias. The rolling lawns, the knolls, the ravines, were richly green.

In his first years there, Dr. Carver had almost lost patience with students who would not keep to the paths but cut across his tender young grass. Then, studying boys and girls as he studied peanuts and sweet potatoes, he solved the problem by watching where the students naturally walked and laying his paths there.

The buildings now numbered one hundred thirty-two, their ruddy brick and white pillars crowning the heights and lining the curved driveways. Some had been built by students, from student-made brick; and though it was now found thriftier to buy the brick, students were still among the workmen as new buildings went up.

The beautiful chapel was Gothic. The library and the science bulding were winged Sphinxes, the hospital was imposing and handsome. Even the natural bowl behind the gymnasium looked strong and able, as if the champion football played by Tuskegee's Golden Tigers had left its traces there.

As it had grown to college standing, Tuskegee had gradually dropped the ''grades,'' which had at first been its main part. Now it had high school, junior college and college, and gave the Bachelor of Science degree in a number of its departments.

The eighteen hundred students showed the change in the times. There were now few boys and girls in patched clothing. Dr. Carver must have enjoyed the look and bearing of these young people and their teachers. He had always grieved over blacks who were ashamed of their color. He had always been quietly scornful of those who shoved and pushed and acted ''up-pity.'' He must have approved of the self-respecting dignity he saw on the campus.

In the beginning the Institute had been mainly industrial. Now the secondary school divided its days equally between vocational and book courses, and college students must give at least six hours a week to trade work, in which forty-one different courses were offered. Majors in Home Economics and Commerical Dietetics had periods of internship like young doctors. And for those who had little money there was still the Five-Year-Plan, by which students spent two years as freshmen, giving an eight-hour day to campus jobs and taking their class work at night.

Tuskegee's third president was now in office. When Dr. Washington died, in 1915, he was followed by Dr. Moton, a distinguished educator, who served for twenty years and was succeeded by Dr. Frederick Douglass Patterson, youthful but well prepared.

Each had served well.

The Oaks, old home of the Washingtons, had been kept unchanged, a campus shrine. Walking through its homelike rooms, tasteful in the somber style of its day, with rich-toned rugs, heavy, dark furniture and good pictures in sepia brown, one could almost see the ghost of the little boy without a name who had slept on a pallet of rags and had never sat down to eat at a properly set table. How far human beings can rise! The house of the present head was as fine, and as tasteful for its day: polished floors and Oriental rugs, bright modern paintings, grand piano, books, glittering lights. The two houses were another index of the general change. Carver Museum was still another, showing the growth of Dr. Carver and of his place in Tuskegee. It was fitting that such a monument should be set up before he died, for he had become the Institute's brightest star.

He had stayed on at the school, refusing princely offers to go elsewhere. An unnamed organization had offered him a salary of one hundred and seventy-five thousand dollars a year. Thomas Edison had offered him one hundred thousand. The money did not interest the scientist, but he must have been a little tempted when Edison urged, "You come with me, and together we will unlock the universe!" Dr. Carver loved Edison, but he could only answer, "I promised Dr. Washington that I would stay on and work for the South at Tuskegee." It did not matter that Dr. Washington was gone, nor that the temperaments of the two had clashed. Dr. Carver had promised.

He also persisted in refusing to accept money for patents or for services. The Peanut Growers had offered him one hundred dollars a month for

Henry Ford (right) was one of Carver's most devoted friends. In 1942 the automotive industrialist presented him with a fully equipped laboratory for food research.

life, for what he had already done for them. He refused this offer, as he had refused countless others. His indifference to money had its annoying side. Like most schools, Tuskegee could have put money to good use, even if Dr. Carver did not want it for himself. But the ''meek Dr. Carver,'' as he was often called, had a core of steely stubbornness that could not be twisted. Besides, a world-famous scientist was not to be dictated to.

He was world-famous. His name was ''in the papers,'' as he had laughingly told his Minneapolis friend it would be. It was in magazines, in books, in *Who's Who in America*.

People flocked to see him. Some were curious sightseers, but many were men and women of importance and of purpose. Ministers came, to learn something of the secret of his nearness to God, for it seemed as if God did indeed work with him, like a Mighty Partner. The Crown Price of Sweden is said to have spent two weeks on the campus, learning agricultural wonders to take back to his country. The Duke of Windsor, while still Crown Prince, visited him with reverent interest.

There were many pilgrimages to Tuskegee from Iowa State, at Ames. One such pilgrim tells amusingly of his experience. When he went to Dr. Carver's rooms, the Doctor was out. While the

visitor waited, he watched an old black man out
front, tinkering with an automobile: a dusty, shuf-
fling old handyman, shabby and dirty from the
work he was doing. The visitor was overcome
with amazement to find that the handyman was
the great scientist he had come to meet.

Henry Ford was Dr. Carver's devoted friend,
and often came quietly, unnoticed till someone
saw his private car standing on the siding at
Chehaw. Ford had been the close friend of two
scientists, Edison and Burbank. After Edison's
death he had put Dr. Carver in Edison's place.
The two men were in many ways deeply conge-
nial, and Ford was the only person who ever
succeeded in coaxing Dr. Carver away from
Tuskegee even briefly for laboratory work. In the
war crisis Dr. Carver did research for a time in
Michigan, probably on synthetic rubber.

Henry Ford named for Dr. Carver an industrial
school for black boys in Ways, Georgia; and he
built a George Washington Carver Memorial
cabin in his Greenfield Village.

As nearly as possible the cabin reproduced Dr.
Carver's birthplace, yet it was probably the most
costly log cabin ever built. Every state in the
union gave boards or logs for its construction.
Short-leaf pine was sent from Alabama, pon-
derosa pine from Arizona, western white pine

from Idaho, apple from Michigan, blue spruce from Colorado, redwood from California, and so through the list, including a mantelpiece of white oak from Missouri, the state of Dr. Carver's birth.

Dr. Carver returned Henry Ford's warm friendship, or he would never have worked for him, even briefly, away from Tuskegee. Not only men, business concerns and colleges had tried to get him away, but even nations. Soviet Russia wanted him to come and help with the agricultural side of their Five Year Plan. Mexican coconut growers, Hawaiian pineapple planters, the West Indies, Japan and Korea, made him tempting offers, all of which he refused. Even when his own government appointed him Collaborator in Plant Diseases in the Department of Agriculture, he accepted only on condition that he need not leave Tuskegee, but should be consulted there.

Years earlier Dr. Carver had received the unusual honor of election to the Royal Society of Arts, in London. Now in his later life similar honors increased. He was awarded the Spingarn Medal, as the most distinguished black person of the year, and the Roosevelt Medal, as the person rendering the greatest service to mankind. The International Federation of Artists, Engineers, Chemists and Technicians chose him as the man of the year who had contributed most to science.

The list of his awards is long and should not be named here.

And at last he was officially given the title which had been since childhood unofficially thrust upon him. His old and beloved school, Simpson College, conferred on him the degree of Doctor of Science. The University of Rochester was so determined to give him the same degree that it did an unheard of thing. Finding that Dr. Carver was too feeble to come to Rochester, the president of the institution flew to Tuskegee and conferred the degree there.

Yes, Tuskegee's lovable old professor had become a great man, and his associates no longer had much success when they tried to tell him what he should or should not do. They would have been glad to advise him about his clothes. Day in and day out he wore a clean old shirt, clean old trousers, baggy at the knees, a coat sweater which he had darned at the elbows, and a shapeless cap. In his laboratory he added an apron he had made from flour sacks. Before he became famous, no one worried about his shabbiness, but now it was different. When he received the proud, the rich, the eminent, or when he went to some grand place to speak, his friends thought he should dress accordingly.

"Doctor," or "Fess," as his closest circle called

him, listened good-naturedly to their arguments, but usually remained firm. When they presented him with fine suits, he merely packed them away with other unused clothing.

"Doctor, surely you will dress up when these big men are coming clear across the country to see you!" the matron at Dorothy Hall would ask despairingly.

He would look at her with laughing eyes and stubborn mouth. "If they want to see me, all right. If they want to see my clothes, I'll take them upstairs and show them a trunkful."

In the trunk was also a handsome fur robe which an admirer had given him but which he had never used. However, one of his richest gifts was not hidden there.

An important person had begged to be allowed to give him a token of friendship. "Isn't there some special thing you'd like to have?" he asked him.

Dr. Carver's reply surprised him: "Yes, I'd like a diamond."

Delightedly, his friend bought him a diamond ring and waited to see him wear it. Again and again he looked for the flash of the gem on those long, strong hands, but he never saw it. At last he inquired: "Doctor, where is that diamond?"

Dr. Carver led him to his mineral exhibit. There

lay the diamond. That was what Dr. Carver had wanted it for.

As to his clothes, on really important occasions his friends could separate him from his sweater, but never, outdoors, from his cap. It became The Cap. Once, when an affair was especially important and he refused to wear a hat, his colleagues bought him the finest silk cap to be had. Then they stole The Cap, limp, threadbare and faded, and triumphantly threw it away. When he was ready to go, and could not find The Cap, the schemers handed him the handsome new one. Doctor scorned it. They coaxed him to the sidewalk, but there he balked. He set his firm, gentle chin and said he would not stir a step without The Cap. They had to hunt it up where they had thrown it and bring it to the quietly waiting owner.

At Johns Hopkins University a great banquet was held in honor of the scientist. It was a grand affair, and important guests stood around in the sleek black and stiff white of dinner clothes, awaiting the guest of honor. Presently two men were ushered in, with a murmur and stir which showed that the expected celebrity had come. One was a handsome chap, formally clad, his spotless collar crowding up his chin in the proper style. That was Dr. Carver's young assistant. The other was a stooped old man, wearing what he called a "durable" serge suit and a large, home-made tie. That was Dr. Carver.

The guests chatted politely, with the slight stiffness caused by dress clothes, while Dr. Carver sat slumped at his ease. In their deep sockets his bright, dark eyes flashed from one man to another, something very like amusement curving his mouth. "He was the only comfortable man there, but soon his easy wit and humor had put the men of the world at ease."

An even funnier occasion was an impressive ceremony at the Tuskegee chapel. The Peanut Growers' Association was honoring the Doctor by presenting the Institute with a relief portrait of the scientist in bronze.

For once Dr. Carver had allowed his friends to dress him in cap and gown and Doctor's hood, and he sat on the platform looking the grand old scholar that he was. He had grown handsomer with age, and now his head, rising out of the velvet-lined, rich-colored hood, was like an Egyptian sculpture. The splendid brow was deeply grooved in horizontal lines, the eye sockets were cavernous, the nose nobly arched. But the Doctor was not feeling so serene as he looked, and he felt still less tranquil when he rose to cross the platform in the flowing majesty of his robes. The folds twisted round his tired old feet and made him stumble. Dr. Carver gave them a kick, and his murmur was audible to those nearest him: ''If I ever get through this, you won't get me into this rig again!''

The Doctor's unwillingness to waste on trifles the little time left to him was noticeable when one of his later awards was conferred, by the Variety Clubs of America. The Variety Clubs have carried on a great work for the underprivileged. They have supported summer camps, hospitals, milk funds, paid for iron lungs, Seeing Eye dogs, ambulances, blood banks. Every year they have helped thousands of children who needed help. And every year they have awarded a silver placque and a thousand dollars to the person whom they have thought the most outstanding benefactor of the year.

In 1941 Dr. Carver was their choice. He was invited to a fine Atlantic City hotel, and there sat on a platform with one hundred other distinguished men. As usual, Dr. Carver was entirely at ease in ''durable'' suit and homemade tie. He had been equally at ease when he entered under a spotlight and to a thunder of handclapping. He enjoyed the occasion; enjoyed the princely service at the hotel; enjoyed rising early and sitting on the balcony of his suite to look out across the bay. Finally he enjoyed his ride to the station under motorcycle escort. Yet he confided to a friend that he could hardly wait to get back to his laboratory.

On all these grand occasions he got a great deal of quiet fun from wearing his plain old clothes. And while his friends kept on trying to dress him up, they enjoyed the joke, too. The sweater and The Cap became symbols, known all over the world, together with the flower in Doctor's buttonhole.

All over the world! The town of Diamond Grove, in the Missouri Ozarks, would once have stared amazed if a prophet had foretold that it would be famous because a slave child had been born in its outskirts. Yet now a tablet and markers proudly show that slave child's birthplace, and the Government has set it aside as a National Monument.

Simpson College has always been a proud school, though small, struggling along with the many other church institutions in that Iowa farming country where learning is so prized. Simpson is rightly proud of the many important men and women among its graduates, but its greatest pride is one lanky black student with a shambling gait, whom it had freely and warmly welcomed after the president of another college had rejected him.

It was a great day for Simpson when Doctor came home to receive an honorary degree. They drove him round the town in a smart blue roadster, and he picked out the places which had meant most to him in those far old days. There was the site of the woodshed where he had lived and washed clothes and sewed on buttons for his fellow students. Yonder was the Liston house, with the bay window where he had spent many happy hours reading. Here were the stores where he had bought the famous dime's worth of corn meal and suet.

"Well, I declare! Well, I declare!" he exclaimed over and over in his unforgettably high, sweet-toned old voice, his face beaming with pleasant memories.

The college had not changed much. Dr. Carver's thoughts flew back to his youth when he entered the same old Science Hall and climbed to the great room under the skylight, where Miss Etta Budd had been his art teacher.

As for Iowa State College, that important school has grown bigger and more important. Splendid new buildings dot the rolling campus, where the trees tower huge and beautiful. The school has illustrious names to its credit, but no other so illustrious as that of their "Mr. Carver."

The years had brought him fame, crowning

him with glory and honor. They had enriched his mind and not dimmed it. They had sharpened his thirst for knowledge and wisdom. They had chiseled his face into remarkable beauty. But they had drained his physical strength.

At length pernicious anemia put him into the hospital. He was a difficult patient. He had been used to activity in every waking minute, and used to doing everything his own way. He could not lie still and be waited on. Even when seriously ill he would jump out of bed to get himself a drink, a book or his whittling knife. The diet prescribed for him did not suit him. His ideas about food had always been definite, and he and the hospital dietitian did not agree. When after some time he was able to leave the hospital, he ordered exactly the food he wanted, with an abundance of wild greens included.

For many years he had lived in Rockefeller Hall, one of the boys' dormitories at Tuskegee. Now it was decided that he should move to Dorothy Hall, the guest house, where a few faculty members had their rooms. It was (and is) a gracious place, built by student labor. It is light and airy, with sweeping staircases and inviting lounges. Most of the many colored paints which decorate its interior were supplied by Dr. Carver from one gulch on the campus.

There Dr. Carver had his bedroom, its furniture painted a strange, soft blue. He had also a sitting room, with his "exquisite elevator" outside its door. The matron of the guest hall could keep a watchful eye on his health, or try to, and the elevator could save his tired old heart the strain of the stairs.

At about this time Carver Museum was opened, giving Doctor a lively new interest to help him get well. This museum was largely brought about by Austin Curtis, Doctor's beloved young assistant. Doctor's story would be incomplete without mention of Austin Curtis. For years friends had urged Dr. Carver to train a helper to whom he could entrust the secrets stored in his great brain, so that they should not be lost to the world. At last he consented to try, and several young men in succession came to help him. They did not fit. He had worked alone all his life, and these green young men bothered him. His mind went back to its work and left them outside, twiddling their thumbs. He could not work with them, and they found it as impossible to work with him. It was not until 1935 that he found the "man he was looking for," Austin W. Curtis, Jr., a recent graduate of Cornell University.

Just as with those who had come before, Dr. Carver welcomed Mr. Curtis and then forgot him. Austin Curtis had patience and initiative. He set to work on some chemurgic problems himself, using the oil from magnolia seed for soap, in place of imported palm oils; making synthetic leather from pumpkins; using waste substances for dyes. His chief especially prized a line of sepia paints which he developed. Doctor named them the Curtis Browns, and used them to paint the personal Christmas cards he sent to friends.

In 1937 Austin Curtis started the museum. This was his second year at Tuskegee and Dr. Carver's fortieth. To mark that fortieth year, money had been sent from all over the country, to pay for a bronze bust of Dr. Carver by a noted Atlanta sculptor, Steffen Thomas. Dr. Carver rather unwillingly appeared for its unveiling, June 2. Though he grumbled that he had no time for such foolishness, he liked the celebration, and chuckled over the suit he wore. It was his college commencement suit, forty-three years old.

People flocked to the festival, and young Mr. Austin thought it would be a good opportunity to give them an idea of the numberless products Doctor had developed. Though Doctor had carried some of these with him on many speaking trips, there were hundreds that had never been seen by the general public.

So Austin Curtis got the use of an upstairs room in the new library building, and there displayed the collection which his chief had kept in the Agricultural Building at the farther end of the campus. Mr. Curtis acted as curator, explaining products and paintings to people who had come to see the unveiling. Among these were many, even of the Institute professors, who now for the first time saw something of the vast scope of Dr. Carver's discoveries. Clearly the exhibit should be a permanent one, and prominently placed.

President Patterson had the idea of displaying it in the outgrown campus laundry. Not only had the Institute outgrown this gemlike little building, but its site, on the main driveway between White and Dorothy Halls, was too prominent for its original use. How fitting that it should honor this intellectual giant who had laundered his way to an education. Throughout the scientist's convalescence he took pleasure in helping arrange in this building specimens of his life's work.

It was something like stepping into a country fair, to step past the bronze bust at the entrance and into this one-man museum, perhaps the only such in the world. At one side were ranged fruits and vegetables which Dr. Carver had canned to show how well they could be preserved. Through the center and around the walls were cases of paints, stains, wallboard, synthetic marble, products of sweet potato, pecan, china-berry, soybean, corn and okra stalks, and so on and on. Here were laces and embroideries, there mats and rugs made from waste string, grass and other fiber. In one case stood a set of dishes shaped and painted like peanuts, which the Negro Peanut Growers had made for him. One corner of the big room was given over to the dumping-ground apparatus of his first Tuskegee laboratory. On the walls were placques and scrolls, tributes from all sorts of organizations. And between the large room and the offices was the art gallery, where the master's paintings were hung. Here were landscapes in the style popular in the eighties and nineties, when he was a college student. Here were also the flower and fruit studies which gave him the deepest delight. They were gracefully drawn, and painted with dewy freshness.

The museum has since been rearranged, after a fire in which all but a few of his paintings were burned or badly damaged, though most other exhibits were saved.

Connected with the museum were a greenhouse where Doctor could enjoy his flowers, and his new laboratory. From this laboratory was set up the Carver Foundation. Its purpose was to keep for the world the discoveries Dr. Carver had made, and to give scientifically gifted young blacks an opportunity to develop their gifts.

Since the failure of the bank in which he had saved his first forty thousand dollars, Doctor had built up another small fortune of thirty-three thousand. This he turned over to the Carver Foundation, adding such sums as the thousand dollars which the Variety Clubs awarded him. Thus, it was hoped, the work could go on as he had begun it.

Contentedly then he worked on, in his rooms in Dorothy Hall and in the museum beside it. His meals he ate in a screened-off corner of the Dorothy Hall kitchen. That was where he wanted them. The Commercial Dietetics Department made Dr. Carver's diet a special project, and a special cook prepared and served it.

Doctor's kindly humor shines out in a ceremony at Dorothy Hall in 1942. He invited a few faculty members and the Dietetics students, and presented a certificate to Emma Fears, a young woman who had been for some time his cook. Another certificate was given to James Lomax, Doctor's cook and friend to his last day.

Occasionally, still, he journeyed to far places to speak or accept honors, but most invitations had to be refused because of his failing strength. As the honors continued without slackening, so did the work, for in spite of all physicians and friends could say, he still went to his laboratory at dawn. In the winter of 1942–1943 he was working for his own pleasure and that of the world on a cross between his favorite flower, the amaryllis, and the Easter lily. He was also busy with the study of new foodstuffs for war use. Of his autumn food bulletins that year a British Member of Parliament had said, "Parliament, when this war is over, should give thanks to Dr. Carver."

Christmas came, and Dr. Carver's room overflowed with gifts and cards from far and near. Many were still unopened on the day when he started down to his laboratory for the last time. In the dark of the winter morning Mrs. Macallister, matron at Dorothy Hall, heard a feeble cry outside the building. Rushing anxiously to answer it, she found Dr. Carver crumpled at the foot of the stair. He had not used his elevator that morning but had made his way down the outside staircase and had fallen.

Tender hands helped him up to his room and laid him in his old Morris chair. There, in a few days, his tired old heart ceased beating. He had worked, joyfully, to the end.

The majestic old body lay in state in the chapel, for sorrowing throngs to see. In his buttonhole was a perfect white camellia. A white woman in Tuskegee had begged to be allowed to give it, from a bush which Doctor had cured for her years before.

For the funeral the chapel was banked with flowers. As the sun shone benignly through the jeweled chancel window, the Tuskegee chapel choir sang some of the great man's best-loved spirituals, and speakers paid him tribute. He had turned the final dial, said President Patterson, and now was fully in tune with the Infinite. He had given to the world a "method and an idea which, if ever fully grasped, will mean peace and plenty for mankind everywhere." These words well summed up Dr. Carver's gift to the world.

Letters and telegrams had come from President Roosevelt, Vice-President Wallace, Henry Ford; from ministers, writers, artists, singers; from countless other notables; and from the simple and humble who had loved "Doctah" and now mourned his passing.

Today, in a grassy clearing near the chapel not far from the Booker T. Washington monument, stands a curved stone seat of classic beauty. Within its arc lies a man-length marble slab with myrtle wreathing it about. This is the inscription carved upon it:

GEORGE WASHINGTON CARVER
DIED IN TUSKEGEE, ALABAMA,
January 5, 1943

A life that stood out as a gospel of self-sacrificing service. He could have added fortune to fame but caring for neither he found happiness and honor in being helpful to the world. The center of his world was the South where he was born in slavery some 79 years ago and where he did his work as a creative scientist.

George Washington Carver: a life of brilliant achievement that "stood out as a gospel of self-sacrificing service."

Uncounted millions of dollars he gave and still is giving to his people and to his country. Health and beauty and high dreams he gave and gives.

Yet his greatest gifts are more than health and wealth and beauty. He proved that the simplest and most distasteful tasks can be a foundation for the loftiest achievement. He proved that he who does the common things uncommonly well can command the attention of the world. He proved that we can make what we want out of what we have.

He proved that a black slave baby who had been thrown away could become one of the great men of the world.

For Further Reading

Adair, Gene. *George Washington Carver, Botanist*. New York: Chelsea House, 1989.

Clark, Glenn. *Man Who Talks with Flowers*. St. Paul, MN: Macalester, 1988.

Lewis, James A. *The Miracle of Dr. George Washington Carver*. Flat Surface, 1987.

Index

Mary (mother), 10–14
Milholland, Dr., 53–59
Milholland, Mrs., 52–59, 61
Minneapolis, Kansas, 35–40
Movable School of Agriculture, 90

Neosho, Missouri, 23, 26–30, 32

Pammell, Dr., 70, 71, 118
Patterson, Frederick Douglass, 135, 151
Peanut, 100, 103–116

Rarig, Chester, 41
Robbins, Clyde, 52

Seymour, Lucy, 33–34
Simpson College, 57–68, 72, 141, 146–147
Simpson, Mathew, 58

Stebbins, Mrs., 75
Sweet potato, 114, 117–118

Thomas, Steffan, 150
Tuskegee Institute, 79, 82, 83, 84–85, 95–99, 117, 119, 121, 122, 133, 136, 138–139, 144, 149–155

University of Rochester, 141

Variety Clubs, 145, 153

Wallace, Henry, 69, 75, 82
Washington, Booker T., 78–83, 85, 90, 96, 99, 108, 135, 136
Watkins, Andrew, 28
Watkins, Mariah, 28–29, 33
Wilson, Jim, 69
Wilson, Professor, 76
Winterset, Iowa, 51–59